THE
AND
THE DEEP

To my family, and especially my wife,
without whose limitless patience and
understanding this book would only
have been a dream.

THE DEVIL AND THE DEEP

A Guide to Nautical Myths & Superstitions

CHRIS HILLIER

Illustrated by
OWEN HILL

ADLARD COLES NAUTICAL

London

Published 1997 by Adlard Coles Nautical
an imprint of A & C Black (Publishers) Ltd,
35 Bedford Row, London WC1R 4JH

Copyright © Chris Hillier 1997
Illustration Copyright © Owen Hill 1997

ISBN 0 7136-4645-4

A CIP catalogue record for this book is available from the
British Library.

Typeset by Chris Hillier
Printed and bound in Great Britain by
The Cromwell Press, Melksham, Wiltshire

CONTENTS

# INTRODUCTION

Many volumes have been written about safety at sea, safe boating and collision avoidance. As yet very few have taken the time to instruct the uninitiated in the finer points of nautical superstition - where to go for information on effective sea-monster avoidance and why *is* it unlucky to whistle while on board?

These days we look at the old superstitions scientifically and smile a little at the old salts and their myths. But if you take the time to imagine what it must have been like for the sailors in the earliest days of exploration, you may begin to realise how they felt when venturing off over the horizon.

Superstition has been defined as the 'science of a pre-scientific people' and it was with superstition that the ancient mariners armed and protected themselves form the great unknown. Superstition was their way of explaining and surviving in a sometimes very hostile environment.

You may have to take the content of this book with the proverbial grain of salt, but to their credit, despite their many fears and superstitions, our nautical forebears helped to shape the world as we know it today.

To quote one of the old authors, 'There is but a plank between a sailor and eternity; and perhaps it is the occasional realisation of that fact that may have had something to do with the broad grain of superstition undoubtedly lurking in his nature.'

 **ALBATROSS** For ages sailors have considered it bad luck to harm these far ranging sea birds. The albatross was immortalised by Coleridge in his *Rime of The Ancient Mariner* and many say that it was this poem that made the superstition so popular.

Contrary to this theory however, it has been said that the assistant navigator on board the ill-fated *Titanic* was called Albert Ross, whom it was rumoured was very bad luck to have around. For decades after the sinking of the *Titanic*, old sailors could be heard to say things like; 'It must have been an Albert-Ross', when discussing the fate of a missing ship. Thus the confusion arose with the sea bird.

Some of the older mariners were not so superstitious however, as many used to make tobacco pouches from the large webbed feet of the albatross, making smoking more immediately dangerous to the health of the birds than to the

Everything's white out there - but it's nothing to worry about.

1

sailor. One albatross was thought to be the cause of a Liverpool dock strike in July 1959.  The ship *Calpean Star* was docked there and was found to be carrying one of these birds which was bound for a German zoo, but when it was discovered dead in its cage it was considered a very bad omen. This, along with the fact that the ship had been renamed by her new owners; labelled her as an unlucky ship; one which any prudent sailor would avoid if at all possible. Superstition not withstanding, the *Calpean Star* was grounded and lost less than a year later. Today the old sailing routes are mostly deserted, so the lonely albatross has more to fear from being accidentally caught in long-line fishing rigs than from non-superstitious sailors.

ALTAR Many of the earliest sailors had a holy place on their ships. The bows of the ship were usually reserved as the altar place, and it was from there that the holy man would offer sacrifices and prayers. Naturally this area was off limits to the ordinary seaman and to be found there would bring severe punishment.

These ancient sailors rarely left home without a holy person on board. There was so much that was unknown about the dangers of the sea that priests were considered as vital equipment on board ship. In the earliest days of sail the marine underwriter was unheard of, so religion was practically the only form of insurance available. The local holy person would be brought along on the voyage (by force if necessary) and it would be his job to keep the vessel safe from storms and sea monsters.

From the altar place in the bow of the ship, the holy man would safeguard the vessel by offering the prayers he hoped would keep storms away from it. The crews of these ships could become quite violent if they met with bad weather and it was said that much of the holy man's time was spent

*Honestly fellas, I'm **sure** I've got the right incantation in here somewhere!*

praying for his own safety rather than that of the ship.

Later, when more was learned about what caused storms, the holy man's position on the ship became more of a decorative one, and he had to move his altar place further aft to leave the bows clear for more important things like the figurehead, and eventually he was left on shore altogether.

AMULETS Amulets and charms have been carried for countless ages by sailors as well as landlubbers. For example, anglers these days will carry their lucky lure along with them or wear their lucky hat. If these items are 'accidentally' left behind, then there's an easy explanation handy for coming home empty-handed.

For the old mariner, however, the amulet or lucky charm was taken very seriously and he would always be sure to have his 'protection' with him, even when ashore. This item could be anything from his knife to a special gift from a loved one. The item in question could provide protection against something specific like drowning, or could possibly be something from the 'cure-all' range that would guard against any kind of bad luck. Sailors were among the first to carry a rabbit's foot, even though these animals were themselves considered unlucky on board. Others would carry a lock of hair from their wife or girlfriend in a small bag hung around the neck, as hair was also thought to have special protective powers.

Other amulets have also included a lodestone or magnet. Many sailors felt that because a compass worked by what to

Obviously not a 'lucky' knife!

them seemed supernatural means, the magnet itself must have special powers.

Gold and silver coins have often been carried as lucky charms and are frequently used in modern day ceremonies on boats and ships all over the world. Coins were thought to bring luck to the bearer. After all, sailors are infamous for being unable to hang on to money, especially when around shoreside grog-shops.

ANCHOR This vital item of the ship's equipment has been considered lucky by even the most unsuperstitious of sailors. For most sailors it represents hope and safety from storms and for many the anchor represents the end of a long voyage and therefore a well deserved rest.

Anchors are probably the most well represented of the nautical icons; they are to be seen on many yacht club flags, boating apparel and even on the sailors themselves. The 'fouled anchor' tattoo is a popular design and is proudly displayed by even modern-day sailors.

There is a story of one boatie who had identical bow anchors on his 45 foot boat, but he always referred to his starboard anchor as his 'lucky' anchor. When asked why the

other wasn't as lucky he simply said that once when he'd had to deploy both hooks in rough weather, 'the starboard had held and the port hadn't'.

I have also been reminded that when you hang an anchor for 'decorative' purposes, it should never be hung upside-down, as the 'arms' of the anchor hold your luck and, if you hang it upside-down, your luck will 'run-out'.

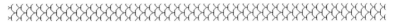

ANGELS Because angels epitomise the 'ideal' woman, they were a popular favourite with the ancient sailors. Spending many months at sea without the benefit of female company often played nasty tricks on the minds of the men who sailed the world's oceans.

Angels and other beautiful creatures occupied many a sailor's idle thoughts. Many ship's figureheads represented angels, and it was to these figures that the old sailors devoted so much attention. Many believed that their ship had a gaurdian angel, and often in times of great peril the crew would imagine seeing this angel on or around their craft, protecting it. At times like these the crew would offer prayers and even some token sacrifices (sometimes a little-liked shipmate) to the angel in thanks for their continued safety.

There are ancient legends, not only in Christian history, of how mermaids and other water-sprites were fallen angels. The general theory was that an outcast angel would be punished by being sent to earth to exist in the sea, and here they would spend much of their time luring ships to their doom and causing other miscellaneous shipping hazards.

These days I'm sure there are more fallen angels in port than out at sea, as many an old salt would testify.

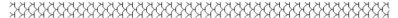

APPARITIONS The stories about apparitions and spectres on or near the sea are probably the most often re-told sea-faring tales. Given the generally superstitious nature of the old sailors, and their fondness for various spirits, it is not surprising that there are tales of ghost ships, ghost sailors, ghost whales, and even the odd ghost fish. These unwelcome visitations were almost without exception a sign of bad luck and in most cases foretold of coming disaster.

The sighting of a ghost ship would often be a sign to the old seafarers that their ship would meet with calamity, and for a

Oh no...Four ghost ships at once! Now I wish I'd joined the army like me Mum wanted!

sailor to see the ghost of another seaman was said to foretell an accident of a more personal nature. Fishermen have also been known to claim to have seen fish that everyone else knows couldn't possibly have been there, so we have to assume there are a great many 'ghost fish' swimming around the world's waterways. Most of us know these fish as 'the one that got away', so to see one is obviously a sign of having had a little bad luck in your fishing ventures.

Apparitions were very common at sea and there are accounts of some voyages where the entire trip seemed to be plagued with sightings of this sort. A man who was a passenger on the *Warratah* claimed to have seen a ghostly figure coming toward the ship across the waves. The apparition seemed to be a warning to him and he left the ship at the next port. The *Warratah* continued on her voyage and soon after disappeared without trace.

These days few sailors claim to see ghosts or other spooks while offshore, but then it may not be just coincidence that the world's navies have abolished the daily 'tot'.

ATLANTIS   The legendary lost continent of Atlantis has been the subject of many shipboard yarns. Sailors tell of how this idyllic paradise on earth was home to more treasure (and more beautiful women) than all the other countries of the world combined. Here in this wonderful land, the winds were always fair, the food was plentiful, and there was always another keg of rum yet untapped.

These stories closely parallel those of 'The Fiddler's Green', which is where many mariners believed they would go when they died. Of course if you had been a wicked person, then your soul was destined for Davy Jones' Locker instead.

The legends of Atlantis were not exactly invented by the old seafarers, as the fables go back to the time of Plato and beyond. Later sailors merely helped to keep the stories alive by retelling and embellishing them as much as possible. Since no real evidence of Atlantis existed, they would often take liberties with these tales; after all who could argue?

Even modern mariners mention Atlantis from time to time, and since the fabled land is supposed to lie in the general vicinity of the Carribean, few miss the opportunity to connect the place with the Bermuda Triangle. Some have said that the lost 'magical' powers of the Atlanteans still exist in the area and this is the cause for the many strange occurences there.

Many modern attempts have been made to locate the lost continent of Atlantis, including Cousteau with his ship, the *Calypso*. Just as the cities of Troy and Pompeii were once only legends, some now believe that eventually hard evidence will surface proving the existence of the legendary lost continent.

Some interesting finds have been made in the sea off the island of Bimini, and while many authorities remain sceptical, there are those who claim they have found Atlantis. An excellent chance for the old sailors to say 'I told you so!'

BAGS (OF WIND) The first reaction many modern sailors have when seeing this heading is to say that they have personally met many 'wind bags'. However this actually refers to a really old superstition and not the guy whose sailing feats increase in proportion to the number of drinks he's had.

During the earliest days of sail it was widely accepted that there were those who could cause a wind to blow at will, in order to help a ship on her way, or even to cause a shipwreck. It was said that some of these weather workers could contain a favourable wind within a leather bag, so that it could be released when needed later.

There was for a time a roaring trade in bags of wind, as many sailors hoped these bags would keep them from being becalmed in the doldrums, an area most sailors look on with dread, even in modern times. These wind-bag peddlars were obviously just the ancient version of con artists, but they actually had few complaints about their stock, as the sailors would often be away for months or years, and would not return to the port until long after the 'warranty' had expired.

After the fleet leaves, we'll take the cash and go into used horses!

As unbelievable as the idea now seems, the concept of being able to control the wind was so widespread that laws were passed prohibiting people from practising weather control, just in case this power should be possessed by the wrong person. These days it would be nice to accurately predict the weather, let alone control it.

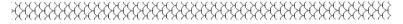

BANANAS This is a superstition that I discovered when out fishing with some new friends for the first time. Someone asked me whether I had brought along any bananas, and being naive to this particular superstition, I wondered if he was after a snack. It was astonishing to learn that not just he but the entire group were quite concerned about finding any bananas.

After it was determined that this wasn't a collective leg-pulling exercise, I found that there was indeed a real

leg-pulling exercise, I found that there was indeed a real superstition about bananas. Apparently if bananas of any type or even a banana by-product is carried along on the trip, it is generally accepted there will be no fish caught that day.

Predictably, after a rather dismal day in the rain with no fish, it was discovered that a caring wife had packed her husband a banana muffin for lunch. Needless to say, I was an immediate convert to this unique superstition despite my initial doubts about whether it was merely a practical joke.

On recounting our poor efforts to others the following week, those who went fishing even only occasionally were all in agreement on the cause; that those who take bananas fishing can expect to catch nothing but a cold.

It seems that this is a fairly widespread belief, and after enquiring, it seems people from many parts of the world have heard of it too.

As 'the jury is still out' on this one, it might be a good idea to leave one particular kind of fruit at home the next time you go fishing.

BAPTISM The baptism of a ship was of paramount importance to the sailors in bygone days. Although most ships are blessed even today at launching, we don't consider it nearly as vital as it once was. Ships were thought to have a soul of their own and if one was to set sail without being properly baptised, it was thought that she would quickly fall into the hands of the devil.

There was a great deal of religious ceremony surrounding the construction and launching of a new ship and at each stage a baptism or other blessing would be held. Baptism was thought to protect the soul of the ship and therefore provide her with divine protection. Men were cautious about ensuring the ship they were sailing on was 'covered' in this way and some would refuse to sail aboard what they called an 'unholy' ship. Religious captains sometimes asked whether the crewmen *themselves* had been baptised.

It is interesting to note that the same men who were so concerned about the baptism of the ship were also quite often the ones who carried lucky talismans and instructed new crew members about ship-board superstitious etiquette. It seems there was plenty of room on board for both religion and superstition, and the two got along together quite well, so long as the practice of religion didn't interfere with any superstitious taboos.

Today's ship baptisms are carried out much more informally and are usually tacked on to the end of the naming/launching speech, almost as an afterthought. It's enough to make an old salt turn over in his grave.

*You're quite sure they've **all** been baptised?!*

BARNACLES Believably enough, barnacles have always been considered unlucky by anyone who has a boat in sea water. The infestation of a boat's bottom by these creatures has always meant slower boat speed, longer passage times and ultimately hours of work scraping.

In centuries gone by, the best antifoul you could get was a good thick layer of copper, and many ships didn't have even that. Any typical seaman could expect to spend a large proportion of his career removing these unsightly blemishes from the ship's undercarriage, and as many who have done the job can testify, it can be a painful exercise. So we can hardly blame the old salts for wanting to label barnacles as unlucky.

Barnacles do have one redeeming virtue however and that is that in times of dire need they are (at least slightly) edible. People who have been stranded on liferafts for extended periods have written that they collected their 'hitch-hikers' for fish-bait and even for food when times got really hard. Some have even said that they might not have survived without them.

Er, captain...haven't seen the copper off the church roof have we?

There are accounts dating back through the 13th and 14th centuries of how many people seriously believed that water fowl such as geese and ducks were actually hatched from goose-neck barnacles. Notable clergymen and 'scientists' of the day claimed to have opened barnacles and found the partially formed birds inside on numerous occasions.

While they apparently took their findings quite seriously, we can't help but wonder to what extent altar wine might have been involved in their studies.

BASIN   There was a belief among many fishermen in the south of England that if a basin was accidentally turned over while at home, disaster would follow. This ill omen would keep the men from putting to sea, as it was thought that the basin was a sort of effigy of the ship. To have your basin turn over was thought to signify that your boat would do the same. Fortunately most modern hand basins are bolted to the bathroom wall, so there remains little chance of this myth interfering with a day's fishing.

Have a nice trip fellas!

Other superstitions involving basins come from the days when it was thought that witches could control the weather. Some sailors believed that witches used large basins of water in their storm raising. They would first float a wax model of a boat or a wooden cup in the basin, then mumble a few appropriate incantations and tip the 'boat' over in the basin, causing the ship to be wrecked.

Basins were not considered bad luck by all sailors, however, because it has been recorded that some seafarers would occasionally attempt to raise a favourable wind for their journey by blowing into a basin of water before boarding the ship. While it seems that sailors felt it an evil act for a witch to raise a storm, it was okay for them to give the wind making a go themselves.

BATHING There was a typical reluctance amongst sailors to go bathing anywhere but in a very shallow bath tub, but when you consider that most were unable to swim, this was only natural. However the old sailors had more than one reason not to go in the water.

Beside the obvious fears of octopi, sharks and the ever-present sea monsters, they had very great fears of exposing their bodies to the elements. To some, entering the sea was almost thought to be tempting fate, as if

It may be unlucky at sea, but if you don't bathe around here, you'll need more than luck!

going into the water with the intent of leaving it again would make the water spirits angry.

As children, many of us were told by our parents not to go swimming immediately after eating as this would give us cramps and make us drown. In the old days bathers would wear 'cramp-rings' when entering the water. These special rings were woven from cords or even flower stems and were often blessed by a priest. Wearing such a ring around your leg or arm was thought to ward off cramps and so bring protection against drowning.

You could almost say they were the old-fashioned equivalent of the more modern water wings, used by children learning to swim. Imagine hearing a mother shouting to her beloved son from the beach, 'Johnny, don't go in without your cramp ring!'

BELLS There have always been strong ties between bells and sailing. Bells were often rung from the town church when the fishing fleet put to sea, or more tragically, when the fleet failed to return. Sailors were the first to wear bell-bottom trousers and they even told the time in bells ie 'four bells', meaning four o'clock.

Taking the lucky bell from yon ship for a wee walkie are we?

Understandably, bells were always considered lucky by sailors, and possibly the original reason for this was that without the aid of the more modern Rolex Submariner, the ringing of the ship's bell was the only way Jack Tar could mark the time until the end of his watch.

Bells have occasionally been stolen from known 'lucky' ships in order to lend good luck to a new ship or to an unlucky one. It has also been said that when a ship sinks, her bell will keep ringing after she's gone. Seafaring tales tell of how on misty fog-bound nights, the sound of a ship's bell can be heard from the site where a ship went down, ages after the tragedy.

There is also a shorebound superstition that if a glass is accidentally struck and made to ring in a sailor's home, it must be stopped immediately. This ringing noise is believed to mock or mimic the ship's bell which would be taken as her 'death-knell' and to let it continue would bring bad luck to the sailor out at sea. While most people these days discredit superstition, it is interesting to note how quickly some will stop a glass from ringing in this manner.
Bells are still found on very modern vessels, and while their presence has very little to do with superstition, they still add an almost mystical touch of old sailing tradition to the ship.

BERMUDA TRIANGLE Many recent books and movies have described the Bermuda Triangle as a haunted, mysterious place. The disappearance of many ships and airplanes in this area is well documented, so to repeat them here really isn't necessary. In fact many people would say that the Bermuda Triangle does not even belong in a book about superstitions, as there are some who believe there really is something strange about this stretch of sea. (Much like the old time sailors held to *their* beliefs.)
From the stories we hear today, you would think that the Bermuda Triangle suddenly formed sometime near the beginning of this century, but there are some much older legends associated with it. As early as 1611, sailors who

visited this area believed the island of Bermuda itself to be inhabited by devils, demons and witches.

There are ancient tales of fierce storms and strange tempests that closely parallel the bad weather witnessed by people crossing through this region in more recent times. Whether there really is anything odd about this area is difficult to say, but you can't help but wonder why this neighbourhood has been spooking people for close to 400 years.

There are other places in the world that are viewed in the same way as the Bermuda Triangle, that is to say, mysterious storms and disappearances are believed to occur there. In the Great Lakes region of North America there is said to be one of these mysterious triangles centred around Lake Superior, which is itself an inland sea, and another near Japan called The Devil's Triangle. Whether we call it superstition or not matters little to those who have experienced these strange phenomena.

That's right Mr President the whole fleet's vanished ...yessir... Bermuda Triangle!

BIRDS   Birds have for a long time been regarded as omens, weather forecasters, bad luck signs, good luck signs and even position indicators. Of all, there is evidence only to prove that they may be regarded as navigation aids, since certain birds can be found flying to or from land at particular times of day.

Many types of bird seemed to appear just before a storm and so they became known as 'storm-bringers', and to spy a curlew, for instance, was thought to predict oncoming bad

It has to be spirit of Fred returned, it can't keep it's mouth shut!

weather. These birds were also thought to cause storms, and to harm one would bring disaster to the ship.

To the ancient mariner, birds held great importance. Most sea birds, for example, were believed to be the lost souls of drowned sailors, and their cries were thought to be voices in torment. Petrels, or stormy petrels, were often called Mother Cary's Chickens. Mother Cary was a legendary witch who caused ships to sink and claimed the souls of the drowned sailors. She would turn them into sea birds so that they could keep watch for ships caught in storms, in order to claim other victims. Mother Cary was eventually banned by Lloyds as a hazard to shipping.

Many of the more superstitious old salts believed in the myth that birds carried human souls, and this is probably why they were very reluctant to harm them. One could never tell if the bird you aimed your musket at was one of your former messmates, and whether he would take offence at being killed twice in such a short span of time.

Many modern-day boat owners still consider birds to be bad luck, but mostly because of the mess they make of the decks!

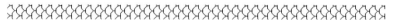

BLACKBEARD   Probably the most famous (or infamous) pirates of all time had to be Blackbeard. Few of his ilk managed to attain the reputation that Blackbeard literally carved for himself in the seventeenth century.

Born in England as Edward Teach, Blackbeard started his illustrious career as a government sponsored privateer. He enjoyed many happy months harassing shipping on America's south east coast, making a name for himself as an evil tempered dangerous adversary.

Of course legends began to grow almost immediately about how 'The Devil', as he called himself, would sail against prevailing winds and currents to attack a poor merchant ship. Since he and others like him were thought to regularly make deals with the Devil in exchange for control over the weather, more normal sailors claimed that they had unholy powers working for them.

Most God-fearing mariners felt that to fall to Blackbeard was akin to being taken by the Devil himself, since it was assumed that the souls of those killed by the pirates would be used as payment for supernatural favours. Blackbeard knew his reputation of dealing with the Devil would strike fear into the hearts of his enemies, so he did his utmost to nurture these myths. It was said that he braided ribbons into his beard and stuck green-glowing slow-matches into his ears when going into battle.

Seeing a six foot four inch, two hundred and fifty pound, red-eyed, green-glowing monstrosity advancing across the deck at you would cause any stout hearted sailor to pause.

Although Blackbeard did his best to claim the crown of the most blood-thirsty rogue on the seven seas, the title might very well have been held by Captain James Morgan. The exploits of Captain Morgan and his band of merry men were already the stuff of legends when Blackbeard was still in nappies.

It almost seems as though Blackbeard may have tried to emulate the career of Captain Morgan, since they both started out as privateers endorsed by the King of England to capture enemy ships, mainly Spanish.

Finding themselves made redundant by inconvenient things called treaties, most privateers turned their natural talents to piracy. Captain Henry Morgan was no exception and made quite a menace of himself, not only with shipping in the Caribbean but often with ports on many of the islands.

Raiding coastal ports in the hope of rich booty, Captain Morgan and his hundreds of followers would burn, rape, sack, pillage and commit all the other unspeakable acts normally associated with pirates.

Such was his success at piracy that Captain Morgan was eventually named Lieutenant Governor of Jamaica. His former atrocities were ignored and eventually he had a rather creditable brand of rum named after him!

BLESSING Blessing a ship these days is usually summed up, when launching, with the words, 'God bless her and all who sail upon her'. To many people this is more than adequate, but some old salts would probably argue the point.

Ships were baptised when they were built and again when launched to protect the 'soul' of the vessel, but there were also frequent blessings held, to 'maintain' this holy protection.

Once a ship had been in the water for a while, regular blessings were held, often when preparing for a long voyage. In fact at any time when the ship's captain or owner felt the craft might need a little extra divine help, one could see a priest or other holy person going about the vessel intoning appropriate prayers and blessings.

Consider yourself a faliure in the blessings department chaplain!

Long before it became unlucky to have a holy man on board, priests were welcomed along on voyages to offer prayers whenever needed. For example, if a ship was passing a headland where bad weather could be expected, a blessing would be offered to keep the ship safe. Similarly, if the ship was passing an area where shipwrecks had occurred in the past, it was thought a good idea to have little blessing said so that the ship might pass unharmed.

Although most modern sailors are not overly superstitious, some still think it a good idea to have their boats blessed by a priest or minister. Yes, I have been told, they can still do 'that sort of thing', if asked.

BLOOD Many ancient civilisations such as the Phoenicians used blood as a sacrifice to the sea, which they thought to be the realm of devils. The preferred type was, of course, human, female, and hopefully virgin. The blood of unfortunate slaves was often used when setting out to capture more slaves, which almost seems like the beginning of a rather gruesome vicious circle.

Sometimes the entire slave was thrown under the ship as it slid down the slipway to the water, in order to 'blood the keel', considering that the slaves were probably the ones who dragged the ship to the water's edge, this seems just a tad ungrateful.

Blood sacrifices were made by seafarers when caught in storms, in the hope that the deities causing the storm would be appeased and save the ship. There are multitudes of stories of how when a vessel was caught in a tempest, some poor crewman would be singled out as a sacrifice and killed to 'save' the others. Usually the unlucky one would already have been labelled as a 'Jonah' anyway and therefore his superstitious crewmates would welcome the chance to 'lighten ship'.

The Romans, Greeks, Vikings and South-Sea Islanders all had their own versions of blood sacrifice, some more ghastly than others. Most of these seafaring races had amongst them sailors who would offer the blood of some

24

other shipmate whenever the going got a bit rough. Often they would offer people who were already dead, which, as long as the various sea-gods weren't too fussy, was at least 'economical'.

Now she tells us she's not a virgin!

BODIES In the middle ages, studies were undertaken to determine whether having a body on board a ship could actually make it sail slower, as was the common belief. Conclusions were varied, but to the credit of the scientists, most results pointed to a reluctant crew being the cause, rather than the body itself.

The old time sailors were very definite in their opinions on having a corpse on board, and for many obvious reasons having one body on board would have posed logistical problems. Given the length of time it would have taken to cross a large area of water in the old days, and the fact that refrigeration was still a long way in the future, having a body on board would have been unpleasant to say the least. Still, this does not explain superstitions regarding corpses.

Around the time the earlier archaeologists began shipping mummies and other artifacts out of Egypt, stories started circulating about how ships carrying these bits and pieces ran into unseasonal storms and other bad luck. It took very little time for the crews on these ships to come to the conclusion that carrying the bodies of old Egyptians was the cause of their strife; that having a body on board was bad luck. There are said to be reports that the *Titanic* was carrying similar artifacts when she went down in 1912.

To have a dead body on board a ship these days is not uncommon at all, though you will never hear the fact advertised in the cruise brochures. It may not be a case of superstition, but having a dead body along would definitely put off the paying passengers.

I've got a bad feeling about this trip!

BREAD There are numerous old superstitions regarding bread and the good luck it can bring to sailors and ships. Many believed that a loaf baked on Good Friday was proof against most marine hazards, yet I have heard it said that when sailing offshore, it is difficult for some cooks to get their bread to rise on a Friday. One can't be sure whether this is due merely to poor technique or whether it has some connection with the old superstitions regarding Fridays. There is also the symbolism of turning a loaf upside-down to represent a ship. Some people in the north of England thought that a ship would be lost for every loaf that was overturned, which is similar to the superstitions concerning basins and buckets.

Some people may recall hearing stories of how loaves of bread were used in rivers to find the body of some unfortunate drowning victim. The usual method was to put a little quicksilver (mercury) in a loaf of bread and put it into the river where the person was thought to have drowned. The loaf was then supposed to float down stream and stop over the body. Accounts from witnesses say that quite often

Things are looking bad, men. Where's that 'good luck' Good Friday bread?

the loaf would 'tack' across or even upstream in order to locate the victim.

Of course a loaf of bread has also been known to make a good sacrifice in times of storms, and Greek sailors have been said to take consecrated loaves to sea with them for this very purpose. If the voyage took a long time, I'm sure the sea gods wouldn't mind if the bread was a little stale.

BROOMS Here is a superstition that few modern sailors would have come across before, but it was common knowledge amongst the old salts that brooms held special powers. It was well known at one time that to throw a broom across the bows of a ship overtaking you would gain you a favourable wind. You can only imagine how many brooms an America's Cup yacht would need to use to keep ahead of the competition.

Most modern boats have a broom of some sort on board (I don't think a 12 volt vacuum cleaner counts) and so if you

Don't leave the church brooms lying about when the fleet's in port!

want a friendly breeze, just hoist it up to the masthead and you will be sure to pick up a good breeze, or at least a few strange looks from your fellow boaties.

Since brooms were said to be the preferred mode of transport for witches, it was thought that the implement itself held magic powers. Some believed that a broom dipped in the water could make it rain, while others thought that to burn a broom would cause a severe storm.

Brooms used to sweep out the local church were thought to be lucky and so would often disappear shortly before a ship was due to leave on a long voyage. In fact the very dust from the church itself would be taken along and scattered around to bring good luck.

Another trick to perform with a broom was to lay it on the deck with the handle pointing in the direction from which you wanted the wind to appear. Somehow, though, it's hard to picture a captain allowing brooms to be left lying about on deck, no matter the reason.

BUCKET Another popular ship board item both then and now is the bucket. There is hardly a boat afloat (nor should there be) without at least one of these on board. I say at least one because it is fairly difficult to spend even a little time at sea without your bucket being at risk of being lost overboard.

For the earlier sailors to lose a bucket was thought very bad luck. Like damaging or losing any part of the ship's equipment, the loss of a bucket would often bring severe punishment, probably for no other reason than that it showed carelessness, a trait for which there was no room on board.

Another superstition associated with buckets was that it was a bad omen to find one overturned. This is similar to the basin superstition in that it was thought to represent the ship, and to have your bucket turn over would be a prediction that the ship would do the same.

To sailors involved in a ship's fire or leak, however, the

bucket was (and still is) irreplaceable. It has oftne been said that nothing moves water faster than a frightened sailor with a bucket.

I once heard a woman refer to a particularly battered specimen of a bucket as her 'lucky' bucket, simply for no other reason than that three newer ones had all been lost overboard, while her 'lucky' bucket was always there when she needed it.

Naturally enough, the lowly bucket has many other uses on board, as it has often been said, 'the head is blocked again; lucky we have this bucket'.

CAT Depending on who you ask, a cat on board can either be very good luck or very bad. I think most people today would say that having a ship's cat brings good luck, provided the cat doesn't provoke allergic reactions. Even if the cat isn't needed to keep the rat population in check, they make good companions, eat little and take up very little space.

There are numerous books by modern blue water sailors who have taken their cats offshore with them. They often tell of how the poor feline would be discovered missing one morning in mid-ocean, and so we can hardly avoid naming these cats as unlucky. Some old salts thought that cats brought the worst bad luck possible, and would throw them overboard, even if one was the captain's pet. Cats were thought to be the familiars of witches, and a black cat in particular would be seen as an evil creature which could not be trusted.

*Oh **there** you are Tiddles!*

31

Older sailing nations thought that cats not only brought good luck but were deities in their own right, and the sailors would make sacrifices to the ship's cat in the hope that it would keep them from harm. Egyptians and Persians took special steps to make sure that the appropriate cat-gods were appeased with offerings and prayers, so that their voyages would be successful.

The ancient Chinese thought that storms were caused by cats, and many of their paintings show cat-like creatures within the waves of storm tossed seas. Many prayers were said from the decks of junks in the hope of being spared from the tempest.

Hope you brought a long scroll? Looks like it's going to be a slow trip.

Aboard other ancient ships, cats were kept almost for the sole purpose of predicting the weather. Many held that the cat's behaviour gave clues to oncoming weather and so the antics of the feline would be well noted. If the cat was seen to be very frisky and playful, the sailors would say 'the cat has a wind in her tail' and this would be a sign that fresh winds were to be expected.

Of course some mention should be made of another type of cat feared by the old sailors. Any seaman who became acquainted with the 'cat' or cat-o-nine-tails must have been very unfortunate. Although the lash was mostly used only as a punishment when a serious breach of ship discipline had occurred, the man involved would still have been considered exceedingly unlucky.

The only modern reference to unlucky 'cats' that you are likely to come across is when monohull sailors talk of the unfortunate tendency of catamarans to capsize when over-canvassed. The usual reply is that '*my* boat may have turned over but at least it's still afloat!'

CAUL   The caul or 'amniotic sac' that is sometimes found covering a baby's head at birth was for many years thought to be the most lucky of good luck charms available. A large number of sailors sincerely believed that the caul would protect them from drowning, possibly because of the myth that it kept the baby from drowning while in the womb.

These items were in very great demand and would be bought, sold, or traded whenever possible. Regular ads were placed in Chicago and London newspapers (amongst others) by sailors wanting to buy these charms. The lucky sailor who managed to procure one would put it in a bag and hang it around his neck, to be continually protected.

It was not only the man before the mast that believed in the power of the caul, as many ships' captains from all over Europe and the Americas kept these charms to protect the ship itself from being wrecked.

This lucky talisman was highly prized by those ashore and at sea alike, and was thought to reflect the mood and health of it's owner. They were inspected regularly and if the caul was found to have changed colour or texture, dire consequences could be expected.

The caul was a highly priced item of marine insurance, as some mariners were willing to pay over $100 for one, which in today's terms would be worth thousands. To some, cauls were more valuable than diamonds, and were often disguised to keep them from being stolen. If only we had known to invest in them.

CEREMONIES Many of our modern nautical ceremonies are in fact direct descendants of very ancient superstitions. The launching ceremony, for example, is today a very civilised affair made up of a small speech, smashing a bottle of bubbly on the bow and then a big party afterwards (the parties have been known to carry on before, during *and* after the launch). This ceremony predates the Romans who launched their ships in much the same way, but originally used Christian blood instead of champagne. The blood was meant to be an offering to the gods of the sea, in exchange for protecting the ship. However, since the Romans always seemed to have a bit of wine handy, this was eventually substituted for human blood. The 'leftover' wine prompted them to start what we know today as the launching party.

Another popular modern celebration is the 'crossing-the-line' ceremony, and this too has its roots in more ancient beliefs. The custom today when a ship is crossing the equator is to hold a mock trial on board and all those who have never crossed the equator before must face miscellaneous imaginary charges.

Someone playing the part of Neptune inevitably finds the miscreants guilty, and they are then sentenced to being sprayed or covered with all sorts of sticky, messy and/or alcoholic substances. (More tame versions are used on luxury liners.)

This ritual was taken more seriously by the old sailors, and in their day, the ceremony quite often involved lowering the accused over the side of the moving ship on the end of a thin line. It was thought that if Neptune forgave the person for their 'crime', the line would hold long enough for them to be brought back aboard again.

Well, use whatever's left and launch the damn thing!

CHILDREN Having a child on board ship was for the old sailors almost always considered a blessing, probably because they would be away from their homes and families for long periods and so to see a child occasionally would be a welcome distraction. Obviously the old salts never had to spend several rainy days cooped up on a 30 footer with four bored kids.

During the numerous occasions when England was at war, the sailors would seldom be allowed to go ashore in case they deserted. So sometimes when in port the sailors were allowed to have their families visit them on the ship. It was not unknown for children to be born on the old fighting ships, down below decks, right between the great cannons. This eventually gave birth to the saying 'son-of-a-gun'.

Due to their innocence, many primitive sailing nations felt that sacrifice of children to their various gods and goddesses

Amazing really, considering he's been at sea for sixteen months!

would buy them divine favours. Fortunately these horrid customs eventually disappeared and were replaced with far less loathsome rites.

It has almost always been a tradition to have young men and boys travel to sea on ships as apprentices and general 'gophers', and it was usually these who featured in some of the less harmful ceremonies. When an important cape or headland was passed, many old-time captains thought it lucky to make a kind of offering to their gods by dunking a young boy overboard on a rope. Whether it actually brought good luck or not is debatable, but we can surmise that it may have helped in the boy's navigation lessons as he would not soon forget that particular headland.

Today many families go out boating together and whether having the kids along is lucky or not is a matter of individual opinion. However, if they can cut bait, do the dishes or scrub the decks, then they must certainly be welcome additions to the crew!

CHRISTOPHER (ST) Saint Christopher is just one of the many saints thought to be a special friend of sailors and travellers in general. It was said that Saint Christopher once helped the young Jesus Christ across a river, and thereafter sailors looked to him as someone who helped people travel across water.

Many statues have been raised in the saint's honour, such as those in Granada and Sicily, so that sailors could offer devotions and prayers to him in the hope of protection. Today miniature statues of Saint Christopher sometimes adorn the cockpits of boats and even the dashboards of cars.

Many sailors thought it was good luck to wear a Saint Christopher medallion around their necks and these became a very popular lucky charm. To lose the medallion, however, was thought to portend disaster, and the more superstitious sailors would take drastic steps to ward off the imminent bad luck. Because many thought that by losing their Saint Christopher medallion they had somehow displeased the saint, they would spend much of their time fervently praying to him, in the hope that they could make amends.

These days, to lose such an emblem is not much of a tragedy, as you can always pick up another at the local trinket shop, and the worst you have to fear is that Saint Christopher will object to being melted all over your dashboard on a hot summer's day.

Poor bugger... the ship's St Christopher statue fell on him!

COLLAR Especially in the days of the great sea battles, a sailor's safe homecoming would be considered rare good fortune, and this eventually led to the superstition that it was good luck to touch a sailor's collar. When a seaman was away for months or years at a time, it was sometimes very hard for their loved ones to accept that they had actually returned unharmed. Many of the more superstitious members of their families would have to actually touch the sailor to make sure he wasn't just an apparition of some sort.

How it came to be that the collar was the luckiest part of the sailor to touch remains debatable, but it is possibly because the sailor would have a little tar smeared there. Many sailors coated their pig-tails in tar to protect the backs of their necks from cutlass blows, and since tar was also thought to be lucky, it was probably believed that to touch a sailor on the collar would double your luck.

A sailor returning home after a long absence would often be approached by complete strangers wanting to touch his collar for luck. As a sailor's first stop when reaching port was quite often the nearest pub, it was to his advantage to tell everyone he was fresh off the ship.

Besides the free pints he might have been given, there must surely have been a pretty girl or two wanting to touch his collar. What better way to meet girls? There are several old superstitions like this one that seem designed purely for the benefit of the sailors themselves, and although it would be difficult to prove, it seems possible that they invented them solely for their own advantage.

COMETS Like most unusual meterological events, the sighting of a comet would bring fear to the heart of many a hardened seaman. Being unable to explain what caused comets or shooting stars, the old sailors would naturally assume that it was a sign from their various gods.

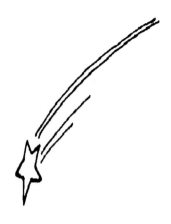

To some sailors the comet was a portent of bad weather, which would take some explaining since the skies must have been clear to spot the falling star in the first place.

To other sailors the comet would be a sign of a coming death on board, as it was believed by some that there was a star in the heavens for every soul on earth, and the falling star meant that someone would soon die.

Many of the ancients took the sighting of a comet as a sign that the world itself was in peril. The rare appearance of Haley's Comet was seen as a terrible occurrence and was thought to signal the beginning of Armageddon itself. Under such circumstances, many sailors wouldn't deem it worthwhile even going down to the ship, let alone putting out to sea.

While today we know much more about comets and what they really are, our knowledge also tells us that if a large comet were to hit the earth, the resulting destruction would certainly make it feel like the end of the world. So, even if the old sailors may not have known a great deal about the study of the heavens, they were right about the potential hazard of comets, if nothing else.

These days, when someone is fortunate enough to see a shooting star, it is usually taken as a good sign and a chance to make a wish.

COMPASS This most basic and necessary piece of ship's equipment has had a long and varied association with superstition. In ages past, when science had not yet explained how the compass worked, many myths developed to explain the compass' almost magical behaviour.

It was generally accepted that the compass needle would point more or less in a northerly direction, but when the needle occasionally varied from north for unknown reasons, the ancient mariners would become alarmed. Obviously anything that could make such a reliable instrument behave oddly must have supernatural powers.

Today regional variation is a well known phenomenon and we can usually compensate for it. Centuries ago, however, sailors became alarmed when on passing certain headlands, their compasses swung wildly. They naturally would attribute this to a devil.

Ye compass be awry who's been eating garlic?!

Different items were thought to cause compass variation and care had to be taken in case they caused the ship to be lost. As much as mariners disliked the idea, now and then a dead body would have to be transported from one port to another and it's mere presence was thought to cause a compass to play up.

Garlic has always been considered to have special powers as well, so it was necessary to ensure that a bundle of garlic was never placed near the ship's compass. So we can imagine that producing charts must have been difficult if the cartographers had to include instructions on avoiding demons and how to compensate for garlic and dead bodies.

COUNTING Counting (if the sailor's education had progressed to that point) had to be carried out with the utmost caution. Superstitious fishermen believed it very unlucky to count the contents of the first net hauled in on a trip, as it was thought that this would be considered presumptuous by the sea-gods. Care had to be taken not to anger the various oceanic deities, as this would spoil the fishermen's prospects for the rest of the trip.

One superstition sometimes observed even today is that it is bad luck to count the miles you have sailed, and then calculate the distance left to reach port. Although it does seem a logical sort of thing to do, to some sailors this is akin to 'counting your chickens before they are hatched', and could mean an abrupt end to the voyage.

Counting boats or ships is also said to be bad luck (I've heard the same about railway cars), and was sometimes cause for punishment on a ship about to engage in a fleet battle. This was possibly because the captains of some ships thought that if a sailor counted the number of ships in an enemy fleet, it would adversely affect crew morale if they were outnumbered.

Counting the boats in a fishing fleet as it left port was also deemed unlucky because in some English fishing villages many believed this would bring ill fortune to those at sea and that the same number would not return.

With modern navigation systems, including GPS, the matter of counting and calculating distances is all done electronically, so if any bad luck should be due, it would surely fall to the silicon navigator.

Gosh! From out here I can see four more enemy ships than I first counted!

CROSS Many ship-board superstitions exist regarding the cross and its particular shape. Sailors in ancient times regarded the shape of mast and yardarm as a great cross, and quite a few hoped this cross would bring divine protection to the ship.

Seamen would often wear a cross hung around their neck as an amulet against accidents, and many believed they were given special protection while working at the 'cross-trees'.

Paintings and pictures almost always portray Columbus' three ships with crosses on the sails, and some historians say this was because Columbus thought it would bring protection to the ships. Since Columbus is given credit with discovering the New World, it could be argued that his ships did have very good luck on their voyage.

Bread was often used as a sacrifice to calm storms, and so it took little imagination for the old sailors to come up with the idea of throwing hot-cross buns into the sea as an even greater good luck charm. Some stories recount how small

*Those buns **may** calm the storm, but don't expect any more for Easter!*

44

pieces of the 'true cross' were carried aboard some ships as protection.

While it makes sense that these items were considered lucky, it is also difficult to imagine where one would obtain a part of the original cross. No doubt, shady characters in most ports would be able to sell you the 'genuine' article if the price was right. (They could also acquire bridges, towers and other well-known landmarks.)

DAVY JONES Few characters enjoy the place in nautical superstition held by the famous Davy Jones. The name is supposed to have two separate origins, the first from the old sailor's mis-pronunciation of devil and the second from Jonah. Understandably, a devil and a Jonah together made up quite a dreadful character to the old sailors, so Davy Jones was someone whom any self-respecting old salt would steer well clear of.

As superstitions went, those involving Davy Jones were very powerful and had to be paid due respect. The most superstitious old sailors thought it bad luck just to utter the name Davy Jones, and would take steps to ensure that others did not speak the name in their presence. 'Speak of the devil

*Well! We think Davy Jones is a **nice** name!*

46

and he's sure to appear' was a phrase frequently heard on the old sailing ships.

Davy Jones was rumoured to seek the souls of sailors, and this is why he was said to create storms and wreck ships. Apart from the innocent victims he claimed, the wicked were said to seek out Davy Jones and trade their souls for fortune and fair weather. Infamous pirates like Blackbeard were often associated with this devil, and many sailors claimed that this is why he and others like him often seemed to enjoy favourable winds, even on windless days.

Davy Jones' infamous locker was thought by most thought to be at the bottom of the sea, and was the place where Mr Jones lived when not whipping up storms and hassling local shipping. Anyone who died on board would generally be buried at sea, and the body would be committed to Davy Jones' locker.

Some say that Davy Jones' connection with the bottom of the sea has to do with the belief that devils and demons habitually live at the bottom of the ocean, so that they may drag down unwary swimmers. Many people believed that Hell or Hades lay deep in the centre of the earth, and that the sea-bottom was an evil place because of its proximity to Hell. This is another example of how people, knowing little of a place, whether over the horizon or under the waves, allow their imaginations to populate it with all kinds of evil creatures.

DAYS   There were many lucky and even more unlucky days in which to go sailing in years gone by. The most 'popular' belief these days is that it is unlucky to sail on a Friday, originally thought by many to be an unlucky day because it was the day Jesus Christ was crucified. Such was the strength of this superstition that many sailors, captains and even merchants avoided sailing or starting a new venture on this day. Modern ports and harbours are as busy on Fridays as any other weekday, but there are those who still feel it is an unlucky day. One sailor I know of has safely sailed tens of thousands of miles offshore, but has had gear failures, groundings and other accidents all on Fridays, and now he avoids leaving port on a Friday if he can help it.

There is an old story of how the British Admiralty once tried to put the old superstition to rest once and for all by commissioning a new ship to be built on a Friday. The story goes on to describe how the keel was laid on a Friday, the ship was launched on a Friday, and was commanded by a Captain Friday. She set sail for sea trials on a Friday and was never seen again! This may be just another story fabricated by British seamen to mock their superiors, but it does show how greatly Fridays were once feared.

The old seafarers had a saying that went: 'Sunday sail never fail, Friday sail ill luck and gale'. Sundays were naturally a good luck day to many sailors because it was the Sabbath, not that they were overly religious as a rule, but because on Sundays many ships' captains allowed special rations to be served. Any day where a sailor could expect an extra serving of gruel with his salted horse meat must surely have been worth marking on the calendar.

Sundays aren't exactly the most exciting days aboard this ship!

Welcome aboard fellas!

DEATH (ON BOARD) The incident of a death on board ship was almost always dreaded by the old mariners. Unless they themselves happened to precipitate the event, the sailors looked upon a death on board as if others would soon follow suit. (During mutinies, this was a distinct possibility.)

Many men would avoid a ship if someone had died aboard because they felt that once death had stalked her decks, the ship would always be an unlucky one. To a sailor, an unlucky ship was to be avoided at all costs.

Many civilisations believed that it was a boat that carried the soul to its final resting place, and so having a dead person on board involved a risk that the ship would become the 'death-bark' and take the entire crew along for the ride.

Some crews believed that when a death occured on board, foul weather would track the ship until the dead man had been disposed of. Needless to say, a big stink would be raised until the burial at sea had taken place.

DERELICT SHIPS To spot a derelict ship, seaworthy and intact would bring to mind the terrible *Flying Dutchman*, feared by sailors the world over. While many floating derelicts may in aspect resemble the the dreaded *Dutchman*, few will dissappear like mist when approached.

Numerous stories have circulated telling of perfectly good vessels being found deserted. Several such stories have come from the North Atlantic where daring crews have ventured too far into the polar ice pack, often looking for the the North West Passage. The doomed crew soon find their brave ship locked in ice, and facing starvation, venture out in search of food.

Although the crews are never seen again, the ships themselves may reappear at any time, sometimes having spent decades entombed in an iceberg. Properly thawed out and not the much worse for wear, the ship will eventually drift south into well travelled shipping lanes, where discovery is almost certain.

Superstitious sailors spotting such a ship could easily be forgiven for being a bit wary and even afraid. While the idea of a sea monster spiriting off the entire crew remains fairly low on the possibility scale, plague and disease have been known to do the job equally well.

Another area frequented by derelict ships is the Sargasso sea a little farther to the south in the Atlantic Ocean. Here ships can lay becalmed for weeks, starving for wind while the crews slowly die of thirst. Long before a friendly breeze appears, all aboard will have perished from thirst and hunger.

When wind does eventually visit these ill-fated ships, and drives them into well frequented seas, there will be few clues left to explain the demise of the crew. Sailors boarding from another ship would find little but sun bleached bones on the decks, yet the ship herself would still be quite seaworthy, possibly still under sail.

Any ship found sailing itself about in this condition would surely make an old salt's hair stand on end.

DOGS There are many who believe, even today, that it is bad luck to see a dog near nets and other fishing gear. Despite the dog's potential usefulness as a guardian while in harbour, many fishermen would avoid having one around the boat because it would spoil the day's catch. One can only suppose that seeing a dog 'cock his leg' over the fishing gear would certainly put off the fisherman if not the fish.

Still, others feel that dogs can be useful as weather forecasters, because being such sensitive animals, they can 'smell' a storm brewing and will howl in the direction from which the wind will come.

Yet another form of dog familiar to many sailors is the 'dog watch'. Having the dog watch has usually meant good luck to many small boat sailors because, falling at around the time of the evening meal, it means that someone else has to do the cooking.

DOLPHINS There are countless tales of how these beautiful mammals have been friendly to, and even helped their shorebound cousins. To see a dolphin leaping at the bow of your ship or boat has always been a welcome sign to sailors.

Then I decided that being nice and good all the time really sucks!

Ancient books tell of how dolphins have saved drowning sailors by carrying them ashore, and even modern stories recount their willingness to help humans. In New Zealand in recent times, a dolphin that came to be known as Opo saved the captain of a fishing trawler, and afterward used to follow his boat when he put out to sea. You can also find a story of how Sir Francis Chichester was saved from sailing onto a reef by dolphins in his book *Gypsy Moth Circles The Globe.*

There are ancient stories of how dolphins were once humans, but were transformed by their own choice into their present aquatic form. Despite the world's problems, it still seems a drastic step to sprout a tail and fins just to escape the world's woes.

DROWNING The danger of drowning has and will always be a real threat to sailors and any others who venture near the sea. In ancient times many sailors refused to learn to swim because they thought that if you fell overboard, it was your destiny to drown, and to attempt swimming was blasphemy.

Still others thought that to save a drowning man would anger the gods of the sea and they would then exact vengeance on the rescuer. Although these excuses are nicely wrapped in religious conviction, we in modern times know that the oldtimers really hated being immersed in water. We also  know why the ship's company was always berthed in the fo'c'sle, as far away from the delicate noses of the officers as possible.

In a not-so-old Scottish tale, the ghost of a drowned sailor, trailing seaweed and dripping water, returns to the ship to rest one last time in his old bunk. His successor, who was sleeping in the bunk at the time, was said to have been startled (to say the least)!

DUCKING Although it was a habit in ancient times to 'duck the boom' and also to 'duck the cannon ball', 'ducking' actually refers to a primitive practice of sacrifice. The earliest form of this ceremony involved chucking the youngest member of the crew overboard when approaching a well known hazardous area, like submerged reefs and sea monster breeding grounds.

Later enlightened captains would merely have the cabin boy lowered by a rope over the side as a 'token' offering. He would then be brought safely back aboard. After all, good help is hard to find!

The act of ducking someone overboard has also, at times, been part of the 'Crossing the Line' ceremony to initiate newcomers to long distance voyaging. Considering the water temperatures around the equator, being heaved over the side in such circumstances might be considered a lucky thing.

ECLIPSE Like many other unexplainable natural occurrences, the appearance of an eclipse would always strike fear into the hearts of early sailors. Naturally, someone on board would have an explanation for the phenomenon, which would usually be a prediction of impending disaster.

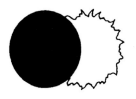

Although the 'technology' to predict an eclipse was possessed by many early civilisations, the appearance of this natural wonder would still come as an unwelcome shock to those out at sea.

To many superstitious sailors, the moon was a goddess to whom sacrifices and prayers could be made for protection from bad weather. So to see a lunar eclipse meant that storms were likely because the moon could not be relied on to provide protection.

Whether or not the eclipse had been predicted, the sailors would dread it's appearance, and even blame the ship board holyman for it's evil portents. Again, to the 'enlightened' would fall the blame for natural phenomena!

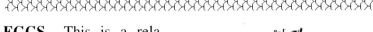

EGGS This is a relatively modern superstition dating from sometime before the First World War, when it became unfashionable to say the word 'egg' or 'eggs' while aboard ship.

Suitable alternatives had to be found and so the terms 'hen-fruit' or 'cackleberries' were used (honest!) when referring to eggs.

Well I suppose that means eggs are off the menu!

There are also those who say it is bad luck to have eggs on board your boat and if given the chance, will jettison the offending produce at the first opportunity. We can hardly blame the old sailors for their beliefs with regard to certain foods because eggs, as with many perishables, can soon make their presence known if left too long at the back of a warm cupboard.

Many a green (new) sailor has been taken aback by being asked how he liked his hen fruit; boiled or poached.

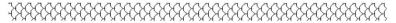

ELMO (ST) Contrary to some reports, Saint Elmo's fire is not what was used to cook St Elmo's supper, but must be one of the most awesome naturally occuring spectacles to be seen while at sea.

Even modern scientific explanations for this natural marvel, do not make us immune to the effects of seeing Saint Elmo's fire.

To the uneducated, superstitious mariners of bygone days, Saint Elmo's fire could mean many things. Old legends explain the appearance of the 'fire' before storms by recounting how the original Saint Elmo died aboard a ship caught in a terrible gale. As he died he promised that his spirit would return to ships thereafter to warn them of coming storms.

When atmospheric conditions are right, the fire will appear in the rigging of a ship and it can behave in various ways. If the balls of fire are seen ascending the rigging, good luck will follow, but if the lights descend, sailors must prepare themselves for severe weather. Other versions state that if the fireballs appear in even numbers it means good luck, but odd numbers spell disaster.

Some sailors felt that if Saint Elmo's fire touched you while aloft in the rigging, it meant that Saint Elmo was calling you to heaven, thus the mad exodus from the rigging when the fire was spotted!

EXTRA HAND The superstition dealing with the so-called 'extra-hand' has little to do with mutated mariners. Stories of long-dead shipmates returning to help handle the ship in times of peril have been in circulation for centuries. Many sailors have claimed to meet the ghost of a friend while aloft during a storm, and told of how the ghost aided in reefing a storm tossed sail.

While we know of the ancient mariner's fondness for a good yarn (and a good bit of rope), there are more modern accounts that also recount visitations from deceased sailors. Although it was close to the turn of this century, Joshua Slocum's tale on this subject is still fairly recent in terms of nautical history.

*Typical! Why do the ghostly extra hands always seem to help **him**?*

Joshua Slocum records how the spectre of Christopher Columbus' pilot from the *Santa Maria* helped him when he was sick, in his book *Sailing Alone Around the World*. Slocum was incapacitated for some time after leaving the Azores, and the *Santa Marian* pilot stayed at the helm of his boat until he felt better. Of course we try not to look too closely at the fact that Joshua Slocum had eaten some very suspect cheese and was also stressed out by a very active goat that he had on board.

Although they require a good deal more battery power, today's extra hand in the form of a tillerpilot or autohelm is probably preferable to the kind that 'go bump in the night'.

EYES Eyes painted on the bows of a boat can still be seen in many Mediterranean and Eastern ports. The reasons given for this 'ornamentation' are that it 'helps the boat to see it's way', or that it wards off the 'evil eye'. To quote one sailor; 'No have eye, how can see?'.

Intensive investigation into some little-known navigation regulations, however, has revealed that painting eyes on the bow of your boat takes advantage of a loophole in the eye exam portion of boat operators' licences in many parts of the world. Thus the crafty use of this superstition by those sailors who are optically challenged!

Yes, they do seem to follow you no matter where you are.

 **FENCES** At one time many people in England believed it bad luck to find a fence barring one's way to the sea. In fact, a parliamentary law was passed to prevent land owners from fencing off access to the beaches. Although we can see how leaving the path clear to the sea-side would be sensible, so that lifeboat crews could quickly aid those in peril, how it came to be a basis for superstition is not so clear. Perhaps sailors, who would often be 'three sheets to the wind' when heading back to the ship, found fences and railings to be insurmountable barriers. Or perhaps with an enraged father or husband behind you, the last thing you needed was a fence in front of you!

FIGUREHEADS To many of the old time sailors, the figurehead was the guardian of the ship; the one who protected her from storms and whose eyes found a clear path around danger. To others she was merely 'that good lookin' wooden lady at the pointy end'.

Those of the former persuasion could be found offering prayers and sacrifices of bread and wine to the figurehead in the hope of continuing good weather. Those others could often be found closely 'inspecting' the curvaceous and often buxom statue, probably because the ship hadn't been to port in months.

Companionship value not withstanding, figureheads were originally meant to embody the spirit of the vessel herself.

Since every ship was supposed to be a 'living' thing, it made sense to have some effigy of that spirit handy whom the sailors could thank when they had good sailing weather. Since kicking the captain's cat was bad luck (for obvious reasons), it also helped to have someone to throw things at if the weather turned nasty.

As sailors grew more enlightened, the figureheads took on more of an ornamental aspect, so ship's captains would often go to great expense to have them covered with gilt and to ensure they were well maintained. As a status symbol, today's hood ornaments on cars are insignificant in comparison.

Of course, the figureheads did not always represent females, as many ship owners and captains thought that a statue depicting one of the multifarious sea gods would be more lucky for, and less distracting to, the men who sailed the ships.

Whenever you're in our port, Captain, cover up the shameless hussy with this!

FISH To list all of the known superstitions dealing with fish and fishing would take a book all of its own. Humans have depended on the sea to provide sustenance since we first appeared on earth, and from the moment we first went fishing we started to accumulate superstitions dealing with fish. When the fish aren't biting, one has plenty of time to sit around and develop theories on *why* they're not biting! Fishing superstitions range from the merely humorous to the outright ridiculous, and often they are as individual as those who go fishing.

Quite often fisher-folk will keep some item with them that proved to be lucky once, such as a lucky lure or even a lucky hat. To many people, fishing is far from an exact science and it's not unheard of to see a commercial fisherman with all of the latest electronic fish finding technology at his disposal, throwing a coin overboard in the hope of a good catch.

There were (and quite possibly still are) people who would throw back the first fish caught on an outing, hoping that more and bigger fish would soon follow. The more pragmatic amongst us would regard this as ridiculous.

*...and remember, humans are **always** bad luck!*

Around the coasts of Scotland there are also those who feel it very unlucky to count the fish as they are caught or to tell others how good their catch was, as this would be tempting fate or tempting providence. Others feel it unlucky to tell anyone *where* they caught their fish, but that's probably because the spot would be 'fished-out' the next time they go there.

FLOWERS You may not usually associate flowers with things nautical, but to many ancient civilisations flowers had special powers, just as today some feel that different coloured roses have special meanings.

Flowers were often thrown after departing ships as a token of goodwill and sometimes even as a form of offering. In the case of Viking raiders, large blocks of stone with flowers carved on them would sometimes be hurled after the retreating longboats, just so that the Norsemen would remember the town they had visited.

Different attitudes have long existed about flowers aboard ships. Some feel they are a gentle reminder of home and loved ones, while many submariners for instance, feel that flowers on the boat are bad luck, as they represent the wreath for a doomed crew.

Through the ages eastern countries have used flowers in various rites and ceremonies. Fresh flowers were often placed about a new ship when it was launched, and basketfulls of petals would be strewn about the decks by the priests performing the blessings, much to the disgust of the sailors handling the brooms!

FLYING DUTCHMAN   Any book dealing with nautical superstitions would be sorely incomplete without mentioning the infamous *Flying Dutchman*. Every seafaring nation in the world has had reports, at some time or other, of a ghost ship, fully rigged and manned by a spectral crew.

The legend of the *Flying Dutchman* says that a diabolical captain named Van der Dekken tried desperately to round Cape Horn, straining his ship and crew to their limits. He swore (blasphemously of course) that he would round the Cape or sail the ship under in the attempt. When an Angel appeared on board to confront him, the evil captain fired a pistol at her and was generally rather impolite. The Angel then condemned the captain (and unfortunately the poor crewmen as well) to sail around the world's oceans for eternity, or until such time as Van der Dekken 'learned some manners'. Presumably they're still out there.

Ghost ships such as the *Flying Dutchman* are almost without exception bad news. To sight the *Dutchman* spells disaster for a crewman, if not for the entire ship. Actual newspaper reports from the 1880s stated that those aboard the ship *Bacchante* encountered a ghost ship that many aboard called the *Flying Dutchman*. Serving as midshipman aboard the *Bacchante* was the future king George. The ship developed rudder trouble, the man who first spotted the ghost ship fell to his death, and when the ship returned to port her commander died of a mysterious illness!

Bad voyage for ghost ships ...eh cap'n?!

63

FOOT This superstition has more to do with the phrase 'putting your best foot forward', than with the traditional units of measurement. Many sailors believed that when stepping aboard your boat or ship, you should always do so right foot first. This probably originated with the old landlubber's superstition that your left side belonged to the devil or that left handed people were the 'devil's children' (a view no doubt frowned upon by the United Left-Handed Persons League).

Just as anything going in a counter-clockwise direction was thought to be evil, stepping aboard a vessel left foot first boded ill for the sailor foolish enough to commit such a transgression. If a sailor stepped aboard left foot first by mistake, he would have to quickly right the wrong by performing a ritual. He should hop backwards on his right foot three times (clockwise) around the mast, and then throw himself overboard. I've personally found that this rite may not actually nullify bad luck, but it will certainly give the 'gods of the sea' a good chuckle.

This 'signing on' may take some time Captain.

GODS The earlier sailors, being more pagan in their beliefs, knew of a multitude of deities from the deep. The more well known of these would have been Poseidon and Neptune, the former being Greek, the latter Roman. In most opinions, Neptune would have been the luckier of the two, having had a planet named after him. Poseidon's name was used for a ship that capsized in a movie and therefore was probably not so lucky.

Ancient mariners were known to squabble over whose god was the more powerful, the Greeks claiming that the Romans stole the whole idea of a sea god from them, and the Romans claiming that Neptune regularly wore a skirt, so what kind of a god was he anyway?

Aside from these disagreements, however, each nation made serious propitiations to their respective gods, such as sacrificing black or white bulls (Is there any other colour?). Originally human sacrifices were made to Poseidon and Neptune, especially on important occasions such as launching, but with the difficulty in obtaining volunteers with the right qualifications (ie *virgin*), animals were often substituted. (It is not recorded whether the animals had the right qualifications or not.)

*Maybe the gods won't miss this **one** sacrifice!*

GOLD Long before overland trading routes were found, ships were the only efficient way of travelling long distances. Since many nations desired trade and the resulting golden profits, they *had* to adopt a seafaring lifestyle. So began the long relationship between ships and the sea.

Gold and ships soon became physically inseparable because many ship builders would nail a gold coin to the keel of a new ship when it was laid, for luck of course. The carpenters always claimed that the coin (provided by the owners) was in fact in place, but since it was in such an inaccessible area, one can assume that many a 'keel-coin' went toward washing down the sawdust at the local pub. It was also common to nail a coin to the mainmast for luck, or as a prize for the crew to strive for.

Being such a precious metal, gold was often used to adorn ships, both as a decoration and also in the hope of pleasing the sea gods. Of course decorating your ship with gold was at one time a good way not only of securing luck for the vessel, but also of dodging taxes.

All's in order Cap'n, except for the small matter of six wayward chests of gold!

HAIR Hair was often associated with luck and things mystical in bygone days. Locks of hair were said to be burned by witches (with poor olfactory senses) in dark rites. Also, a lock of hair from a loved one was often carried in a bag around the neck for good luck.

Sailors too had superstitions regarding hair, and it was not unheard of for a sailor to forbid his wife to cut her hair while he was away at sea. Given that many sea voyages could take months or even years, this superstition was definitely one that would test the wedding vows.

Many seafarers seriously believed that to cut your hair (or your nails) at sea during a calm would raise a storm, while others felt that it was safe to do so *during* a storm, which according to the former group, was already too late! Still, anyone who had the time for personal grooming during a storm was probably not in close touch with reality, and so was probably better off out of harm's way.

*'Er ole man's away on one of them **long** voyages.*

Best tell our young artist friend the crew don't much like sea blue hatches.

HATCHES To turn a hatch cover over on deck was often thought to make a mockery of the ship and that the poor vessel herself would soon follow suit. Just as turning over a basin or shoe would bring similar disaster, upturning a hatch was definitely bad luck. If the bosun accidentally steps into a hatch that you have left open, the ship may not sink, but he'll make you wish it had!

Similarly, to paint a hatch cover blue was also thought to mock providence and if it was turned over, the boat would do likewise.

Sailors always had to beware of any ship's component that might be seen to mock a vessel and cause it to turn over. Many, when caught out, gave this excuse for not putting the lid down on the loo!

HOLY WATER   These days, most sailors haven't easy access to a 'cup 'o' holy water', but many ancient navigators thought that you could not safely leave port without this precious liquid.

If perhaps the local holy person himself was not available, it was thought advisable to carry a dram or two of holy water along just in case. Ships' captains carried it along in bottles marked specially marked 'to be used in emergency only', and it was poured on stormy seas in the hope that it would calm the tempest.

Despite many old Scottish beliefs, holy water was ordinary well water that had been blessed by a priest and *not* by a distillery, and so it was thought to be more effective in calming the seas and not the nerves.

Seems to be a lot of 'Holy water' coming aboard Chaplain!

...and here comes the 'Let's get a lucky horseshoe before we sail' crowd.

HORSESHOES The reasons for thinking that an old horseshoe is good luck have been lost in antiquity, but sailors as well as landlubbers believed in their special powers.

Although horses themselves were seldom permitted aboard ship, except perhaps salted and in barrels, the shoes from a horse were always welcome aboard as talismans.

It is said that the most well known of English sea heroes, Horatio Nelson, ordered a horseshoe to be nailed to the mainmast of his flagship *Victory* when sailing to the Battle of Trafalgar, 'just in case'. Unfortunately for him, it was one of his last orders. England won, but alas, he came home preserved in a barrel of rum.

IRON This superstition is bound up with an old myth that claimed 'cold iron' was the bane of witches and other evil doers. 'Hot iron', on the other hand, was used to press the captain's uniform and it was a very unlucky sailor indeed who was assigned this duty, as it was said that some captains would flog a sailor who missed a wrinkle.

There was a belief that since iron was a man made material it was anathema to witches who gained their powers from elemental forces. Therefore if you thought you were under the influence (of an evil spell), all you had to do was touch cold iron, and you would be protected.

Other forms of iron familiar to the old sailors were when the ship failed to tack and was 'caught in irons', or when criminals were 'clapped in irons'. Either situation could be considered as unlucky!

You'll need even more luck if you don't get orf our gun mate!

71

JONAH The original Jonah was of course the one supposedly swallowed and then regurgitated by a whale. The reason for his having been swallowed by the cetacean to begin with was to do with his lack of faith in God, so to start with it can be said that it may be bad luck to be an atheist.

But, aside from the origin of the term 'Jonah', sailors began to call anyone whom they considered bad luck by this name. For example, comments like the following could often be heard: 'That Albert Ross* is the worst kind of Jonah, and the Cap'n had no right to risk the ship bringin' 'im aboard'.

Of course not all those labelled as Jonahs were really bad luck, but the old sailors often needed an outlet for their fears and so sometimes even someone whom they *knew* to be 'innocent' would still be singled out.

Once you were labelled as a Jonah you would aways have to watch your back. With very little provocation, your ship mates might decide they were better off without you and throw you to the fish! *see ALBATROSS*

*'scuse me ma'm, did you just say 'Have a nice trip **Jonah** boy'?!*

KEEL The laying of a ship's keel was a grand and momentous occasion for many ancient seafarers. Because the keel was thought of as the vessel's backbone, and the vessel itself was considered almost a living entity, the beginning of the ship's life was given due respect.

Naturally enough those who had commissioned the ship to be built had an investment to protect, and therefore would sometimes consider it prudent to enlist the local priest or holy person to bless the keel. Others throughout the ages have come up with diverse rites for protecting the spine of a new craft. Some Scotsmen, for example, would attach a red ribbon to the first nail driven into the keel and many other boat builders nailed a gold coin to the keel. Of course there are also tales of human sacrifice by the more gruesome civilisations (if they can be called civilised) relating how bound slaves would be trapped beneath a keel as it was laid.

Modern fibreglass yachtbuilders being a rather pragmatic lot, have sensibly avoided all the inconvenience of these superstitions by building the keel and hull as one intregral unit. And labour laws being the way they are would make the practice of some of the more ghastly old superstitions difficult to say the least.

Anyone checked into this shipowner's religious affiliations?

73

KNIVES A sailor's knife was quite often his most valuable (if not his only) possession, and to many seafarers, it represented his status aboard ship. Of course the mere fact that he owned a knife would make a sailor a lucky man, but knives were often thought to have special powers.

Most sailors would own the same knife for years or decades and so would form a great attachment to it. To lose a knife was always thought to be a great misfortune and would cause strife among the crew if it was thought to have been stolen. Due to the constant threat of being entangled in various ropes, a sailor had to make sure his knife was always handy, and he'd be unlucky indeed if he didn't have it when he needed it most.

Such were the superstitions surrounding knives that they were used as talismans. The most common belief concerning a knife's power was that in order to gain a favourable wind, you only had to stick your knife into the mast in the quarter from which you wanted the wind to appear. This may or may not have worked in the old days, but we can't help but wonder how it would work with a modern metal mast!

You have a very confused crew Captain!

Avast mateys! I'm too busy for those old Kraken jokes!

KRAKEN The old timers used this name for many mythological creatures, but the origin seems to have originated with the giant squid or possibly the giant octopus. There exist many accounts of giant squid attacking ships and having great battles with sperm whales, such as those mentioned in Sir Francis Chichester's book, *Along the Clipper Way.* The size of some of these beasts has been estimated as being in excess of 360 feet from tentacle tip to tentacle tip, with diameters of the 'arms' being more than ten inches. Little wonder that the old sailors dreaded them!

According to ancient tales a kraken was a fearsome beast that could pluck a sailor clean off the deck of his ship even while under way, and many a sailor learned to fear these creatures, despite the fact they had never seen one.

Old salts would retell these ancient stories to the new hands in order to instill a proper respect for these creatures. In order to suitably impress one's fo'c's'le audience, one should never let the facts get in the way of a good yarn!

Some old mariners say that trying to outsail these monsters, which could move at great speed, gave birth to the term, 'kraken on more sail', but then some old mariners have been known to have a sense of humour!

LADDER To pass a flag or the ship's colours through either a ladder or steps aboard a sailing vessel in the old days was a dire omen. Aside from the fact that it might trip up the captain as he was coming down the steps (a *very* bad omen), it was thought to predict the fall of the ship.

Especially in the old wooden fighting ships, breaches of even superstitious discipline like the mishandling of flags would often be dealt with by raising the offender instead of the pennant to the yard-arm.

This old superstition surrounding the ladder aboard ship probably derived from the even older myth that anyone passing under a ladder while ashore would be hanged.

Modern sailors find ladders a blessing when working on their boats ashore, but never call it a ladder if it's used to

You've achieved a 'triple whammy' Len!

76

enter the saloon of a boat from the cockpit. There are still skippers who consider such poor terminology a capital offence!

LIGHTS (AT SEA)   There are many tales of lights seen at sea, told by sailors the world over. One of the more easily explained sources of light seen even by modern mariners is the natural phosphorescence created by tiny creatures living in the water. When a vessel passes through the water, the wake created disturbs these little animals and they give off a cheery greenish glow. In ages past, sailors seeing this for the first time naturally assumed their ship was being followed by some supernatural force.

Modern sailors who have sailed at night will be quite familiar with this phenomenon and most find it enchanting if not actually romantic. Relatively recent stories from offshore sailors describe how their boat has passed through large areas of this type of light, that seemed to stretch as far as the eye could see. While scientists find it difficult to explain such disturbances, we can imagine that the old sailors must have thought their ship was plying a sea of fire.

Stories of spectral lights hovering over the water at night are common the world over, and most tales hold that the appearance of these lights foretells disaster. The story of the *Palatine* on the American east coast has been retold many times and recounts that spectral lights in the shape of a burning ship appeared regularly to predict severe weather.

There was a story from 1942 of two airmen who had survived in a rubber raft after their scoutplane had been shot down. Adrift for some time, they managed to kill an albatross for food, (a dire omen to say the least!). During the night their superstitions must have got the better of them when the skin from the bird glowed bright green! Of course they knew little about how the albatross feed on many types of luminescent sealife, and so the eerily glowing bird was quickly thrown overboard. Once again, those at sea learn the perils of killing an albatross!

77

MAELSTROM   The great maelstrom or whirlpool most often said to exist off the Norway coast, has in fact been seen at various points around the globe. Ancient mariners who had travelled a great deal often surmised that it was in fact the same whirlpool moving about and possibly even following some 'Jonah' aboard their ship.

The Norwegian maelstrom has been the subject of much conjecture over the ages and many theories have been put forward as to its cause. Early Norse legends said that the whirlpool was actually the boiling kettle of a sea-god named Hymer, while others said it was caused by a hand-mill carried by a maiden who had drowned in that spot.

Vast swirling masses of water have been known to engulf small ships and so these maelstroms were feared and avoided whenever possible. Sacrifices were sometimes made to appease the god or demon causing the whirlpool and we can certainly imagine many sailors on bended knee when one was sighted.

Scientists were always ready with a 'logical' explanation for such natural occurrences and a one-time popular theory was that the Norwegian whirlpool was actually caused by water rushing through the centre of the earth. This theory held that the waters of the world were usually out of balance and so the maelstrom was necessary to shift water from one side of the globe to the other.

Other well educated people scoffed at this 'plug hole' theory as having been invented by someone who had spent too long in the bath. Any theorist worth his salt knew that whirlpools were caused by the giant lampreys that live at the base of these maelstroms.

Since superstitions at sea are not confined solely to the sailors of bygone days, modern ship captains will sometimes avoid these seemingly haunted places. Of course small boat owners steer well clear of these areas as well, but since they may be in *real* danger, we may forgive them!

MARY CELESTE Probably the most famous of all sea mysteries is the story of the *Mary Celeste.* Built in Nova Scotia and launched in 1861, she began her career under a cloud when her master became deathly ill on her maiden voyage and died within a few days. Originally given the name *Amazon*, which was unlucky because it began with the letter 'A', and then having her named changed, which was even worse, made her an unlucky ship three times over.

On November 7th 1872 the *Mary Celeste* sailed from New York, bound for Genoa, Italy. Five weeks later, the very seaworthy *Mary Celeste* was found abandoned about 600 miles west of Gibraltar, but with no sign of the crew. The captain, his wife and two year old daughter, plus seven crewmen had vanished without trace. The total lack of evidence pointing to why the crew abandoned a perfectly good ship in mid ocean prompted numerous theories to be put forward.

Superstitious old sailors blamed everything from sea monsters to demons, yet since more than a century has passed, it appears as though the *Mary Celeste* mystery will remain just that!

MERMAIDS   Next to sea monsters and evil apparitions, mermaids were probably the most popular myth to occupy an old sailors' mind. Many a lonely sailor, starved of female companionship, has imagined he has seen a mermaid. These creatures are usually said to be a combination of buxom female from the waist up with a long fishy tail from the waist down.

Real sea creatures have often been taken for mermaids, and numerous sailors have mistaken a sealion for these beautiful mythical beings. As well, it is said the manatee has tricked many a sailor's eye into thinking he's seen a mermaid. We can only surmise how long a sailor would have to have been at sea to confuse a manatee with the female form!

Of course not all mermaids were said to be benevolent, and it was quite often said that they would use whatever charms they had at their disposal to lure unwary ships into dangerous waters. Ancient tales often blend the stories of mermaids and sirens together, so that sirens possessed the mermaid's form and the magical charms necessary to wreck ships.

Such were people's fascination with mermaids, that many seaside carnivals and travelling exhibitions featured supposedly real mermaids. Just to prove his theory that there's a sucker born every minute, Barnum had a crude version of a mermaid on display in his show in the mid nineteenth century. Being made up of an ape's body attached to a fish's tail, it was a great crowd pleaser, and was eventually put on display in the Boston Museum.

Despite the ancient origins of this myth, people in modern times have also been captivated by the idea of mermaids. Much romanticised in books, movies and even cartoons, the mermaid seems destined to remain a part of human history.

MOON   Sailors in most sea faring countries believed to varying degrees that the moon had special powers. Many thought the moon to be a goddess and so (you guessed it) would make sacrifices to her in the hope of good weather and prosperous voyages. Others thought that the moon could accurately predict coming weather, and Shetland Island fishermen had a popular saying regarding her weather forecasting abilities: 'If you can see the moon clearly, then it will rain soon; if you can't, it already is!'

The sailor's preoccupation with the opposite sex is infamous worldwide and so when the new moon's tips seemed to point upward the sailors sometimes said: 'The horny moon is on her back, mend your shoon and sort your thack.' Modern dictionaries don't define exactly what a shoon *or* a thack is, but I'm sure the old sailors knew it meant that the moon was predicting bad weather.

MUSICAL INSTRUMENTS Like many of the humble possessions of sailors, a musical instrument, even if it was hand-made, was thought to be almost irreplacable. As music when it was well played seemed to hold special powers, then the instruments producing the music sometimes seemed magical in themselves.

Mariners only had their own talents to rely upon for entertainment, so the owner of an instrument was usually a welcome member among the crew. Several stories from the late 1800s tell of how a sailor played so poorly that his mates threw him overboard, on the pretence that he was a 'Jonah', which meant for him that his instrument was an unlucky one.

One instrument became famous in it's own right when Sir Francis Drake died and his drum began to play seemingly of it's own accord. Sir Francis may be long gone, but it's said that Drake's drum is played by invisible hands whenever England is threatened.

Honestly guys, I'll take lessons!

NAMES AND RENAMING Many modern sailors as well as old salts have their favourite superstitions regarding the name and naming of their craft. Of course the most well remembered one is that it is very unlucky to rename or re-christen your vessel. Many examples can be given of how grief has come to a ship after being renamed and one of the most popular of these is the story of the *HMS Victoria*. This unlucky ship, while on manoeuvres in 1893 (it *is* an old story) collided with another war ship in mysterious circumstances resulting in an horrific loss of life.

Of course many old sailors would say that she was doubly unlucky because her name ended in the letter 'A'. Any ancient mariner worth his salt could tell you that to give a vessel a name ending in the letter 'A' is very bad luck. Many claimed that the *Lusitania*, lost on May 7 1915, was a perfect example of this superstition at work.

The worst trouble you could get into these days by renaming a boat would be if you mis-spelled your wife's name while painting it on!

Owner's always changing lady friends.

NARWHAL   The narwhal has quite unintentionally generated many myths. The male of this cetacean species grows a tusk or tooth from it's upper jaw that sometimes reaches up to eight feet in length. This hollow horn is spiral shaped and is made of high quality ivory.

Given the fact that these whales are rarely seen outside of arctic waters it is somewhat surprising that their tusks could give birth to so many tales. It is said that the vikings first brought the narwhal's horn to Europe, and closely guarding it's origin, they helped to start the myth of the unicorn.

To kings and nobles, the horn of a 'unicorn' was a powerful talisman that, aside from healing and aphrodisiac properties, had the ability to protect against poison. Given that kings were under constant fear of being poisoned, they were quite willing to pay large sums to possess one of these horns. In the mid 1500s two of these supposed 'unicorn' horns were used to pay a debt equal in modern terms to $1 million!

The myths about these horns persisted for hundreds of years, almost to the end of the nineteenth century. Big game hunters regularly returned to England from Africa claiming to have stalked and shot the fabled unicorn. Of course, only those familiar with the rarely seen narwhal knew the truth!

There are others who believed that the narwhal was once in reality the unicorn but, having missed the boat when Noah left in his ark, they were transformed into their present form. This type of 'instant evolution' was also said to have turned some humans into dolphins.

Those more familiar with these creatures have their own ideas about the narwhal. People in Iceland believed narwhals would surface in front of a ship that was doomed to be wrecked, and those in Greenland thought these animals were the embodiment of doomed souls.

Modern sailors and fishermen of northern waters may at times scoff at the old unicorn myths, but many still believe it bad luck to harm the narwhal. The unicorn may be extinct, but the modest animals that started all the fables are still protected by their *own* superstitions.

NOOSE There were a few superstitions regarding the use and tying of a noose on ships in the old days. Many felt that it was bad luck to tie a noose, as death would soon follow (figure *that* one out!). Some naval institutions still forbid anyone to tie a noose, even for 'fun', because of some very musty old laws regarding mutinies.

If, however, one should be called upon to tie a noose, it had to be done properly, and tied with *thirteen* turns anti-clockwise, or 'widdershins'. This combination and number of turns was meant to ensure that the soul of the 'hangee' went where it was intended, straight to Davy Jones' locker!

We finally get the noose just right and they let him off with 200 lashes!

 **OIL** There has been a large difference of opinion in yachting circles as to whether pouring oil on the water during a storm will prevent waves from breaking aboard. Many have tried this trick and whatever the effect, little *bad* luck can result from spilling some oil overboard, unless of course you happen to be a petro-chemical company executive.

In ancient times oil was poured on the water to calm a storm, but since only a few drops were employed, the act was more religious than practical. Understandably, the ancients had little or no access to nicely refined fossil fuels, so other types like olive oil would be used. Some captains would have their holy person place a small container of this oil in the waves, along with the appropriate prayers, in order to calm a gale. If the said holy person was accidentally swept overboard in the attempt, his prayers would certainly be all the more earnest!

*Honestly! I'm **sure** it's working. (I hope!)*

PIGS There are few modern sailors who have to concern themselves with having pigs on board and their relative 'luck' value, but in days gone by pigs were very bad luck indeed. On long ocean voyages the old mariners would often ensure they had enough food with them by bringing it along 'on the hoof'. That is, goats cattle and other barnyard citizens would be kept in pens on deck for eating at various stages throughout the journey.

Pigs, however, were often left behind by many sailors because of the strong superstitions surrounding them. Some say this was because pigs or swine were related to the devil and to even say the word 'pig' while at sea would presage disaster.

Sailors also thought it unlucky to meet a pig on the way to the ship, and such a meeting would be used to explain any bad luck encountered after getting under way. The more modern pragmatic sailor would be hard to convince that his new racing yacht had just run aground because the helmsman had seen a pig on the way to the yacht club!

She might reckon meeting you was bad luck when I gets her to the butcher.

This isn't the same Timmins who blasphemed God and all His angels
just one port tavern ago, is it?

PRAYING The sailor's close relationship to the sea and it's multifarious deities meant that he often got in a lot of practice at praying (especially in the hurricane season). During the middle ages, Arab and Barbary corsairs would pray for fair winds, but when their own attempts failed, they would beat their Christian captives to pray for them. No doubt such a practice did little to endear them to their *own* gods.

Today's sailors have at least this much in common with their nautical forebears; you can often hear people say, 'God, if I live through being seasick, I'll never go to sea again!' Of course, we humans being the forgetful lot that we are, would disappoint most deities by thanking our lucky stars instead of recognising supernatural assistance.

PRIESTS The relationship between priests or other holy people and sailors has evolved dramatically through the ages. Initially when the world's nations went to sea, it was almost unheard of to travel without at least one priest on board because of the belief in their ability to call on divine protection for the ship. Ages later it became quite unlucky to have a priest sail with you and they were as unwelcome on board as a pig or a rabbit.

Since sailors were so superstitious regarding the dead, they thought that priests, who have much to do with ministering to the dead and dying, would not be 'wholesome' shipmates. Besides they weren't likely to be very lively company when visiting shoreside pubs and other establishments that cater to the whims of seafarers.

Nowadays of course attitudes have changed, and since priests can drink and tell off-colour jokes as well as the next person, they are welcome aboard any boat or ship.

Well...they ***have*** *to sail with us because they're missionaries and this is a mission ship!*

PUDENDUM Here is a superstition that may require an old dictionary to help the reader understand it a little better. Several old texts refer to the practice of patting a pudendum for good luck before heading out fishing or setting out on a voyage. This was once known as 'touching the bun' and although it's difficult to put a finger on the reason for it being lucky, many thought the action would bring them luck. Perhaps it's simply because a sailor found himself in the situation where he *could* carry out this practice, that he counted himself lucky.

The origin for this one may be obscure, but given a little publicity it could make a comeback!

*Are you **sure** they have to do it for good luck?*

RABBITS Like many of the animals sailors took exception to, rabbits were held in fairly low esteem by seafaring folk. To mention a rabbit while at sea or to bring one on board would throw many old mariners into fits. In fact many sailors referred to them as 'ground pheasant' in order to avoid saying the word 'rabbit'.

Unless the rabbit had been separated from it's feet and the fluffy paws used as lucky charms, most would have nothing to do with a rabbit or hare. Just like other superstitions where the origins have been lost in the mists of time, the reason for sailors disliking the poor, misunderstood rabbit is no longer clear to us nowadays.

Many old superstitions originated when one accident or misfortune was associated with some other unrelated incident. (Superstitious minds don't deal well with the concept of coincidence.) We can only surmise that ages ago some sailor tripped over a bunny on the way to the docks and did himself an injury. Then suddenly rabbits became bad luck.

So it's give the ocean cruise idea a miss then, is it Peter?

RATS It may be hard for modern people to understand, but rats were once considered good luck to have on board ship. Only when they were *abandoning* a ship was it thought unlucky as demonstrated by the old adage, 'Like rats from a sinkin' ship!'

Many said the rats would leave an unlucky ship before it left port, to avoid going down with the rest of the crew. Others say it's because they simply couldn't tolerate the cooking.

Having rats on board the old English fighting ships was thought lucky, where they were known as 'millers' because they often got into the flour. The crewmen on these ships found that rats made excellent pets, weather forecasters and appetisers. The ships' companies were never fed very well and so the rats were highly prized meal supplements, having been quite well fattened on the food in the holds.

I reckon we must be the luckiest ship in the navy, Harry!

REMORA   A remora is a suckerfish that attaches itself to other fish (or to boats) via a sticky disk on top of its head. Old time sailors knew that the remora could sometimes grow to be as large as its host, and that they sometimes attached themselves to a ship. They then deduced it must at some point get to be as large as a ship, and so they gave this unassuming little fish the lofty title of 'ship-stopper'.

The slowing force of these fish was so well known that not-so-old dictionaries still give *remora* as a definition for something that creates an impeding effect. While not exactly gullible, the old mariners tended to believe readily in supernatural causes for unexplainable occurrences. If a ship was making poor time due to an unknown current, it wouldn't take long for the sailors to start looking in the water astern for the tell-tale 30 foot fins of the dreaded ship-stopper.

Nein, Mein Kapitan, ve haven't any bright ideas!

SAILS Sails were the only motive force available to the old wooden ships and so had to be treated with due respect. There was almost always a sailmaker on board, or at least a member of the crew who could effect repairs to the sails - sort of the equivalent of today's marine engineers.

Due to the awe with which their skills were regarded, these fortunate individuals were held in high esteem by the rest of the ship's company. The sailmaker had to ensure, however, that he was cautious in the exercise of his art, for many supernatural traps awaited him. Certain types of stitching were thought to be lucky, probably because they held better than others, wheareas using 'an unlucky stitch' would bring disaster to the vessel.

Also the sailmaker had to watch that he didn't change the types of stitching in his sails, because if he mixed different stitches they would become jealous of each other and pull out!

The prudent sailmaker also had to make sure he never sewed sails on the quarterdeck, as this was considered bad luck. The quarterdeck was the domain of the officers, so to have them stumbling about over sails would hardly increase the sailmaker's luck quotient.

Early on in the voyage, sail maker Sid realised they were a very superstitious crew indeed.

SAINTS There were almost as many favourite 'sailing' saints as there were ships at one time. Each little fishing village or port had it's own patron saint and a chapel devoted especially to him or her. The prayers offered to a saint in times of trouble would sometimes seem to be answered with a miracle, and so the sailors would adopt that saint as their own.

At one time in England, there were over 370 chapels devoted to St Nicholas, who was one of the more favoured of maritime saints. St Nicholas was looked to for protection, not just by English sailors, but by most European sailors. One can only assume he responded more quickly to prayers than other saints. With over 370 chapels, there was sure to be a 'branch' nearby!

Today's sailors still have their favourite saints and if pilgrimages are anything to judge by, they are extremely popular. Among the more popular saints are St Kitts, St Lucia, St Tropez and St Maarten, all of whom seem to prefer warm climates.

The rest perished Vicar. Please refund our pre-voyage donation to the chapel!

Flea plague or not, stop scratching. We've already too much wind!

SCRATCHING There was a popular belief among European sailors that if the wind had deserted you a good scratch could get you moving again. Now, scratching some itchy part of the anatomy might provide a little relief, but would do nothing to help move the ship along. This superstition refers to taking a nail (preferably made of iron) and scratching the mast in the quarter from which you wanted the wind to blow. Similar to sticking a knife in the mast, it was thought that the interaction between metal and the mast would invoke some supernatural force to cause the wind to blow.

Many sailors disagreed as to which mast it should be (should your vessel be blessed with more than one), the mizzen or the main, but most would try it at least once when becalmed.

Modern sailors should beware of trying out this superstition however, as the inflated price of marine varnish makes scratching the mast an expensive experiment.

SEAGULLS   Numerous old superstitions have been observed about seagulls and their relationship with those who go down to the sea in ships. Due to their mournful sounding cries, sailors have long believed that seagulls (and other sea birds) embody the souls of drowned sailors, and therefore many held that it was bad luck to kill a seagull. Yet others thought that certain parts of the gull, like it's wings for instance, could be used to calm the wind and so would carry these as talismans.

Fishermen used to think that seagulls would bring them luck at fishing, and even today they use the gulls to help spot shoals of fish. Fishermen ancient and modern also held that to spot seagulls flying inland meant a storm was rising, and would quickly head their boats for shelter.

Modern boaties regard seagulls in the same light as they do barnacles. Between the mess below the waterline and the mess on deck we are kept so busy cleaning up after these nuisances there is little time for sailing. Some ancient mariners may have thought them special, but anyone who has had to scrub sun-dried gull-dung off the deck would hardly call themselves lucky!

That be the returned soul of O'Grady, the practical joker!

No one believes in us anymore. We've got to change that!

SEA MONSTERS Sea monsters and sea serpents occupied almost as much of the earlier navigator's thoughts as did mermaids and other female forms. A great fear of the unknown coupled with a good dose of ignorance helped to create a monster in the shadow of each wave. Many of the earliest marine charts had areas labelled 'Here There Be Serpents', and although contemporary sailors don't believe in monsters, charts should still label some high-priced marinas in the same manner.

A popular theory at one time stated that tides were caused by the slow breathing of a large (it would have to be) sea monster. An extrapolation of this concept would have to be that storms were caused by the monster sneezing. Many ideas were advanced about the possible size and location of the sea serpent, but as no one was willing to go and check, hypotheses supported by nice, safe calculations soon took over.

Sailors were often recruited from rural areas and so had no knowledge of the sea or its inhabitants. It would take little imagination for a young lad to turn a whale into a sea monster, the size and cruelty of which would grow with each pint at the pub back home.

SHARKS Shipwreck was not an uncommon occurrence in the early days of sail and so sailors had first hand experience of the ferocity of sharks. These fearsome predators would often follow a ship for days at a time and so, naturally, many superstitions developed around their presence.

One of the most popular beliefs was that to see an odd number of sharks around the ship meant there would soon be a death on board. Some claimed that sharks could smell death and would follow a ship where there were sick men or a dead body aboard.

Sharks being the scavengers that they are, they would probably followed ships because they liked the quality of the scraps being thrown away.

South sea islanders thought that sharks were the embodiment of various sea gods and therefore would offer sacrifices to them. To others, wearing a shark's tooth necklace was thought to protect the wearer from attacks by sharks and even from drowning. Still, the difficulty in obtaining the teeth might have been very similar to the old landsman's adage; 'who will bell the cat?'

No, you go ahead. They give me indigestion!

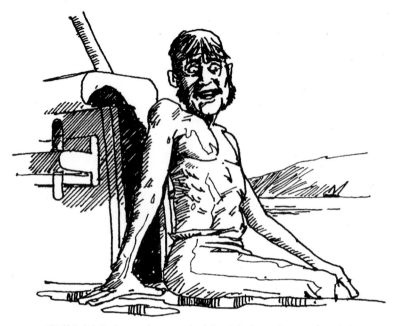

Well I didn't drown, but somebody's nicked me shoes and socks!

SHOES When a sailor was fortunate enough to possess a pair of shoes, he always had to ensure that they never landed upside-down on the deck when he took them off. There were many who thought that a shoe resembled a ship (because you travelled in it?), and so if your shoes turned over so would your boat.

Another superstition observed by people near the seaside was, that it was a good idea to place your shoes and stockings in the form of a cross when you took them off to go swimming. Although many sailors wouldn't or couldn't swim, those that were brave enough thought the cross formed by your shoes and socks would save you from drowning by averting cramps (ye olde crampe).

When working on a ship many sailors went barefoot, especially when up in the rigging. Bare feet allowed better purchase on the foot-ropes and so if a sailor did slip whilst wearing shoes, obviously these would be his 'unlucky' shoes.

Oh my! The gods have miraculously turned my silver coin to copper!

SILVER This noble metal, being more easily attainable by sailors than gold, was often prized for its superstitious value. Not only was silver thought to be the bane of werewolves, but witches were said to dislike it as well. Since it was thought that witches had nothing better to do with their time than whip up storms at sea, it was considered a good idea to carry a silver trinket or coin with you to ward off evil spells.

If a storm did arise, the knowledgeable sailor had only to brandish his silver talisman at the seas and the storm would abate. Of course if it was a particularly persistent storm, the silver might actually have to be thrown in, but this step was taken only in the direst emergencies.

Most sailors recognised the similarity between a shiny silver coin and the full moon. It was thought that the goddess of the moon controlled the seas (they were closer to the truth than they knew) and so to have a silver coin as a talisman would bring good luck.

Although they may not know that it is to please the moon goddess, many contemporary sailors still place a silver coin at the base of the mast for luck when stepping it.

SNEEZING The origins of this superstition are buried so deeply in the annals of marine history that they may never be unearthed. To theorise slightly it might be said that some believed sneezes were caused (for reasons of their own) by witches or the devil. Sailors thought that if you sneezed while boarding your vessel, you had better try to sneeze to your starboard (right) side and not your port (left) side.

Since the left side was thought to be connected with the devil, sneezing in this direction would give the devil aid in bringing disaster to the ship. So if you sneezed to your right side it could be taken as a good omen for all those on board.

We can only assume that timing your arrival at the ship with a well-placed pinch of snuff could guarantee a prosperous voyage!

Not a great idea, this pepper cargo!

SPIDERS It sometimes seems amazing that even when a boat is moored far from shore, spiders still find their way aboard. You can remove them and their webs regularly and they will reappear as if by magic. Perhaps boat builders secret them in special, hidden places as good luck charms. One explanation may be that many sailors think it bad luck to kill a spider (it will make it rain) and so they throw them overboard. The little arachnids will drift with the tide or current until they fetch up against the neighbouring boat and, thankful for a safe voyage, will soon happily set up house. Spiders are seldom actually killed, we just trade them from boat to boat!

The new hand turned out to have arachniphobia.

SPITTING   There are many actions that a sailor can perform on a vessel to change his or her luck. Spitting to windward has always been unlucky, but at least it's good for a laugh for your shipmates. Spitting (or being sick) to leeward or downwind is definitely the recommended direction.

Old salts may also tell you that it's bad luck to spit on the deck, and besides lacking social delicacy, it's a slip hazard. In the old fighting ships spitting on the deck was usually rewarded with the punishment of having to scrub said deck, all 1500 or more square feet of them!

Other spitting superstitions imply that it's bad luck to spit over the bow at the beginning of a voyage, and that it's good luck to spit on your fish hook before casting.

It is said that some South American fishermen will spit chewed coco leaves on a hook to help their fishing.

Many people know of (if not actually practice) the ritual of spitting on your palm and shaking hands to seal a deal. The more squeamish may wear gloves.

STOLEN GOODS There were many who believed, aside from the legal implications, that it was lucky to steal from other boats. Many fishermen felt that to steal hooks or a net from a lucky boat would transfer the good luck to them.

There have also been ship builders who would steal a small piece of timber from a known lucky boat to build into their vessel. This act was supposed to bring them good luck, but imagine what an up-to-date lawyer could do with a lien in such a case!

Stolen boats and ships however will almost always bring

bad luck to the thief. The theory here being that it was the true owner who had named and christened the boat to bring it luck. If that vessel is then taken without permission, the vessel herself will punish the miscreant by sinking with him on board.

Tell me again how you came by this wee sinking boatie!

SWIMMING For a variety of superstitious reasons, the average sailor had quite an aversion to immersing himself in water. Some claimed that to go swimming would tempt the sea spirits and that thereafter they would hunger for the swimmer to return (which probably meant that the claimants simply didn't know how to swim).

When a person did get up the nerve to go swimming however, it was always said they should wet their head before their feet, as the feet were considered inferior to the head. To go swimming in the nude was thought by many to be very beneficial and good luck would befall the swimmer. If you should happen to see someone of the opposite gender swimming in the nude then there is no doubting your good luck.

Of course a sailor on his way to the ship who spotted a pretty girl swimming in the nude was immediately said to possess great good fortune. If no actual good fortune resulted from the encounter, at least he would have an entertaining story to tell when away at sea.

Captain McDonald was very succinct when the crew took an interest in starting swimming lessons.

TATTOOS Tattoos are almost synonymous with sailors and the stereotypical old salt will always be festooned with body art. Tattoos these days are applied mostly as a statement of personal taste, but sailors in bygone days read a lot into each tattoo that they wore.

Many sailors felt that it was good luck to have a cross or some other religious symbol tattooed on their body in the hope of holy protection when out at sea. Many others would forego carrying a lucky charm and just have it indelibly etched on their skin. They are much more difficult to lose that way!

There were also those who felt that a properly applied tattoo was a good form of identification, should they be killed by some misfortune. Even today many seafarers find themselves the proud owner of a new tattoo after a good night on shore. Of course bad luck will certainly befall any sailor who can't remember his lady love's name whilst in his cups!

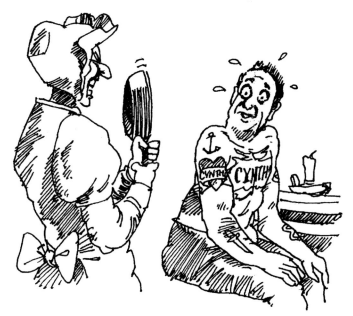

So! Who's Cynthia?!

107

Not too late to renew the captain's insurance is it?

TEMPTING FATE To tempt fate or providence was one of the worst crimes of superstition imaginable to the old time sailors. This type of superstition is alive even these days because sailors still refer to their destination in obscure terms, stating, 'we are headed for...', rather than 'we will be at...'. To give your destination in definite terms is thought to be taking God or other supernatural powers for granted, and so you will be made to pay for your audacity.

Just as farmers have the addage 'don't count your chickens before they're hatched', fishermen would say nothing of their catch until it was landed safely at the market. To count your fish or even estimate the number you might catch would spoil your luck for sure.

THIRTEEN The number thirteen has been considered very unlucky by Christian sailors for ages. You will seldom see the number thirteen painted on a small boat and many would refuse to sail if the crew numbered thirteen.

It is said that the stigma surrounding this number dates back to the number at the table for the Last Supper and that, combined with a Friday (the day of the Crucifixion), it is a disastrous number. Hence the common fear of Friday the thirteenth.

One story that appeared in an old sailing text claimed a Scottish fisherman found himself in a predicament when he caught thirteen fish in his net at the end of a rather unsuccessful day. He was distraught at having to keep such an unlucky number of fish, yet it was such a miserable catch, he was reluctant to throw even the smallest fish back. He resolved his problem by cutting off the head and tail of one fish and returned to port with twelve and one half!

Mentioning she's our thirteenth ship will not exactly help our sales and marketing drive!

Knowing he still had 2 hours to low tide, Billy's friends entertained themselves.

TIDES There are many old superstitions concerning tides, yet few are ever heard of today. One of the more common old superstitions was that a person could not die until the tide was low, as referred to in Dicken's *David Copperfield*; 'People can't die along the coast except when the tide's pretty nigh out'. If you manage to 'hang in there' until the tide turns, then you've got at least until the next tide.

Another myth observed by many midwives was that male children were born at high tide, and girls at low tide. Today the rhythms all seem to have changed and babies are born seemingly at random, in total disregard for ancient traditions!

These old superstitions seem to bind the life and death of humankind with the slow pulse of our environment, something that perhaps the ancient mariners understood better than we.

TREASURE   Always close to a sailor's heart was the idea of treasure. The pursuit of gold and wealth was the reason many nations put to sea, and why many men took up a seafaring life. Probably the greatest stories of treasure come from the Americas, where first the Spanish looted Inca gold, and then pirates harried merchant ships for rich cargoes.

Tons of gold and gems were taken from Mexico, and the Spanish treasure armadas did not always make it home with their priceless freight. Stories of sunken galleons and buried boxes of loot have circulated around the warm waters of the Caribbean for ages, and of course treasure hunters have flocked there in the hope of making a quick fortune.

There is the story of one fortune hunter who sailed to the Gulf of Mexico searching for treasure and quickly came away with a small fortune. Unfortunately for him he had gone there with a large fortune, proving the theory that more money has been spent looking for the loot than has ever been recovered.

Naturally enough ghosts figure greatly in treasure stories and it was due mainly to the pirates that these yarns became well known. Pirate leaders knew of the superstitious nature of their followers and would often kill a man and bury him with the treasure, knowing that most sailors would assume the ghost of the murdered man would haunt the scene. The famous captain Kidd was said to have done such a deed on an island named Appledore Island, where ghosts were regularly sighted, supposedly guarding his treasure.

South of New Zealand a ship named the *General Grant* was wrecked while carrying gold to England. Treasure hunters who travelled there soon after the ship sank were frightened off by ghost ships, which many sailors claimed was the *Flying Dutchman*. Salvage attempts in the area were often plagued by accidents, and divers have met with tragic accidents there.

Treasure attracts many, some living and apparently some not. It would seem that some spooks feel that if they can't take it with them, then they won't leave!

I said 'Don't turn to port' - to your left! This is your left hand - Oh Bloody Hell!

TURNING When turning your boat or ship, it was always thought bad luck to manoeuvre in an anti-clockwise (counter-clockwise) direction. Just as certain numbers had connections with the devil, so too did the anti-clockwise direction, sometimes called 'widdershins'.

The clockwise direction is a natural movement for right-handed people, but left-handers were thought to be associates of the devil, because their natural direction was anti-clockwise. Left handed helmsmen were constantly finding themselves in hot water!

To turn your boat anti-clockwise was thought to mean that you were turning to the devil, and so your ship and soul would belong to him. It is a good thing in many respects that we are less superstitious than the old sailors, because being afraid to turn anti-clockwise in a crowded yacht basin could land you in a lot of trouble, if not a law suit!

WATERSPOUTS As is the case with many natural and awesome phenomena, the ancients came up with their own explanations and cures for the occurrence of a waterspout. Many said that the waterspout was a great dragon that dipped its head into the sea to drink and such was its thirst that it sometimes sucked up ships and men by accident. Not a malevolent animal, just severely dehydrated.

Another explanation for a waterspout was that it was caused by a demon beneath the sea and that it was sent to overcome the ships in the area. (What *wasn't* a demon sent to destroy ships?)

Despite their not-too-accurate explanations for waterspouts, the sailors in ancient times had as many cures for them. Besides praying, which we can be sure was done in a very earnest manner, they would throw vinegar at them and sometimes brandish black-handled swords at them. Another cure was to fire a cannon into the column of water, in the hope that the noise would frighten the spirit away.

Waterspouts, as with tidal waves or *tsunamis,* are best not viewed from sea-level. If you have the bad luck to see one, it may already be too late!

WELL, THAT DISPROVES THE VINEGAR THEORY!

WAVES Any surfer worth his salt will tell you that waves come in sets, usually in predictable numbers like seven or nine. Being able to time the sets allows them to catch the best waves for the longest rides.

This belief in ordered numbers of waves is hardly a new one because deep water sailors have believed in the concept for ages. Some held that the ninth wave or the one immediately following it would always be larger than the others and were often called 'ship-killers'.

These nicely predictable waves only had to be carefully watched to ensure they would not engulf the ship. If it appeared that the wave would break over the vessel, one only had to make the sign of the cross at it and say a quick prayer to avert disaster.

Only those who have tried this can testify as to its efficiency, but in times of trouble even small comforts are welcome!

The ninth wave

Bad weather coming captain!

WEATHER   Ages before the invention of the weatherfax or weather satellites people had very little other than local knowledge to help them foresee oncoming weather. This was usually restricted to comments like, 'If you can see them hills it's going to rain, and if you can't it already is'.

When venturing out beyond their own neighbourhood, mariners had virtually nothing to help them predict or explain the weather, so they had to develop their own methods. What they observed immediately prior to any change in atmospheric conditions was generally ascribed as the cause for that change. For instance, if the captain's steward had just spilled a bowl of hot soup into the captain's lap and then a squall hit the ship, every time thereafter when the steward did this, the crew could expect a squall. But such primitive forecasting methods seldom work for very long as 'accidents' generally happen to people like clumsy stewards.

The myriad methods for projecting coming weather varied from ship to ship, but occasionally the mariners would strike upon a method that actually worked. Curiously enough these usually involved watching sea birds or mascots.

WHALES The cetacean was no more exempt from the superstitions of mariners than any other creature of the deep. Many sailors, who had probably grown up on a farm and seen nothing larger than a cow would have been awestruck at the sight of a whale surfacing near the ship.

The earlier sailing vessels were surprisingly diminutive and so to see an animal as large as their vessel quietly glide past would surely have 'put the fear' into many inexperienced sailors. Whales and other large natural creatures are surely the basis for (most) sea monster stories.

Even when they were better understood, superstitions still followed the whale, as Melville amongst other writers recorded how it was believed that whales could transport themselves vast distances. It was sometimes said that whales, including the famous Moby Dick could be harpooned near Greenland and then reappear in the South Pacific. One supposes they had not yet applied migration theory to whales!

Believe in sea monsters now do we?

116

Following seaman Yate's unsolicited whistling of 'Let's Be Happy', a great tempest scattered the fleet and sank four vessels!

WHISTLING This is another old superstition that modern seafarers may be familiar with. Many of us have heard that whistling on board a boat or ship can raise a storm. The usual reason given for this is that one or two of the more irritable sea gods will think the whistler is mocking the wind.

Of course mere mortals should never mock any element, and to do so will bring supernatural retribution. Nevertheless, if you should find yourself becalmed, you may whistle (very quietly) to try to raise a favourable wind.

It is not only other-worldy powers that take exception to whistling however, as at one time the British Admiralty made it a punishable offence to whistle on board a naval vessel. It's not that the Admirals greatly feared the old superstitions, but that whistling was once used as a signal in a mutiny!

Certain shoreside establishments gave some comfort to superstitious sailors by calling themselves the 'Pig and Whistle', both strong taboos while aboard ship.

Don't anyone say a thing!

WINDS Modern sailors can occasionally be heard complaining about the wind. It usually deserts you altogether when you need it most or it blows half a gale when all you want is a gentle zephyr. We have at least this in common with those who first went to sea ages ago, that the wind is just as unpredictable now as it was then.

The old time sailors used to think that to mention the breeze was a sure way to kill it. For example to say, 'What a lovely breeze there is blowing!' is the most unfailing way to either stop a wind or cause it to blow from the wrong quarter. NEVER talk about the wind.

The early sailors had probably never heard of Mr Murphy, but they would be familiar with the idea behind his first law of sailing. Murphy's law simply states that no matter which direction you wish to head in, the wind will blow from that quarter!

WITCHES Included in the ancient mariner's guide to explaining weather and other natural phenomena is a large section on witches. Many sailors were familiar with the concept that witches had control over the weather and so could wreck ships at will.

Two women were arrested in England in 1716 for being witches. It was said they had taken off their shoes and by using their feet to make a lather of soapsuds, had raised storms and wrecked ships. They were probably just washing their feet!

Shakespeare knew of the power of witches to control storms, as he had the three witches in *Macbeth* devising various means to wreck shipping. This was a well known belief in sixteenth and seventeenth century England and a state paper from that time told of a large pack of witches that had been rounded up, some of whom were 'of good ability'!

In hindsight we can't help but notice that the supposed storm brewing activity of these alleged witches always seemed to increase at certain times of the year, in autumn and winter for example!

*Where have I gone wrong?! She **likes** ships and refuses to sink them!*

Darling, I'm sure the winds have abated enough now!

WOMEN Last but certainly not least are the superstitions regarding women on board. Again this is one that many modern sailors will have heard before. The superstitious mariners who held to this belief were mainly fishermen but also those aboard long distance naval and whaling ships. Many fishermen thought that to meet a woman on the way to the boat was a bad omen for the day's fishing, especially if the woman wore a white apron or was barefoot.

Aboard long distance ships the men would be away from home for months and often years at a time, seldom touching in to port. Sailors being sailors, for a woman to be present aboard would cause obvious problems with morale and discipline. For that same reason though, pregnant women were often welcomed by the crews.

Again, sailors being sailors, most believed in the superstition that it was lucky to have a *naked* woman aboard, because everyone knew that when she bared herself, her presence could calm the wind. Many a ship has been lost in calm weather!